1,000
SPANISH
IDIOMS

1,000 SPANISH IDIOMS

J. Dale Miller
Brigham Young University Press
Provo, Utah

Library of Congress Catalog Card Number : 71-180253
International Standard Book Number: 0-8425-1513-5(p)
Brigham Young University Press, Provo, Utah 84602
Printed in the United States of America
10 9 8 7

CONTENTS

FOREWORD

A noted Romance scholar, Dwight Bolinger, has said that the essence of syntax is freedom. When a group of words like "how do you do" become frozen to each other and resist normal syntactical substitution (there is no *how do they do, how will you do, where do you do,* and so on), the result is not a typical phrase or sentence of the language, but an expression we designate as an *idiom*. The traditional definition of an idiom — that the meaning of the whole expression is not derivable from the conjoined meanings of the constituent parts — suggests that idioms are, in effect, "complex lexical items." Like other lexical items, they must be learned individually, preferably in a meaningful context, by a student who hopes to master the language.

But dictionaries seldom include idioms in any consistent way as entries. Some idiomatic expressions do appear as subentries under one or more of the so-called content words (equivalent to listing *disease, mistake,* and *descent* as subentries of *ease, take,* and *scent*), and some depend on a made-to-order definition of a constituent word (*kill* defined as "pass aimlessly" because it appears in the idiom *kill time*). The bilingual dictionary is even less likely to be helpful if the idiom is a longish expression in both languages (*go to the extreme* translated by *pasársele a uno la mano*).

Yet to really know a language one must know and be able to use its idioms, or at least the common ones. Fowler points to idioms as "a manifestation of the peculiar," by which he refers to that part of a language which is characteristic and individualizing. To know the bare structural and lexical form of a language without a meaningful control of appropriate idiomatic usage is to be acquainted with the mechanics but not the essence, to know the skeleton but not the spirit.

Why does the study of idioms not receive more systematic attention? Many reasons, no doubt. One may be that they are so common. Some idioms are "over-successful metaphors," easily converted into clichés, whose use is considered a weakness that many teachers traditionally avoid. But for the student idioms cannot become trite until they first become familiar, and if the student is to share the native's feeling for what a cliché is, he must become overfamiliar. In the context of language learning in the classroom, this implies systematic study of idiomatic usage.

The present collection attempts to meet the student's need with a significant compilation of Spanish idioms, listed in the order of frequency of usage, and therefore presumably in the order of usefulness to the student. The list is constructed with care and method, to include the expressions most widely present in international usage in the Hispanic world, and therefore most appropriate for the study of Spanish in the United States, where students need a broad linguistic and cultural base. The presentation is convenient, clear, and well illustrated (both contextually and graphically). Translations are appropriate for level and register, maintaining both the denotative content and a relevant feel for the surrounding context.

This volume will be welcomed as a useful supplementary tool by teachers who wish to improve the effectiveness of their efforts to impart meaningful control of the language to students who need to learn Spanish for real use in the real world.

J. Donald Bowen
University of California
Los Angeles

PREFACE

While serving as Foreign Service Institute Regional Language Supervisor, Middle America, for the Department of State, I came into very close contact with the Spanish spoken by foreign service officers, staff personnel, and Peace Corps volunteers. Not only did I have a chance to observe them performing in a Spanish-speaking environment, but I was also expected to evaluate them and make recommendations for their improvement.

The Problem

One of the frequent difficulties Americans had in using Spanish was their inability to understand and use idiomatic expressions. A Peace Corps volunteer, for example, was heard to say *Está tarde, vamos a la punta* for *It's getting late, let's get to the point* — usage which might easily be misinterpreted since *está tarde* could mean *he* or *she* (instead of *it*) *is late* and *vamos a la punta* literally *let's go to the point* — point, in Spanish, referring only to a physical location such as a tip, an extremity, or a sharp end. Had the volunteer known two commonly used idioms, *hacerse tarde* and *ir al grano*, in place of *está tarde* and *vamos a la punta*, he would have made his point clearly and precisely without incurring the risk of misunderstanding.

Obviously, no student can memorize all, or even a substantial part, of the vast number of Spanish idiomatic expressions. An effort needed to be made to find a manageable number of the universally used idioms of everyday speech on which students could first concentrate.

Antecedent Research

After a survey of the available sources of Spanish idiomatic expressions, I found most lists were compiled of expressions arbitrarily thought to be most common. Only one list had been published using frequency of occurrence as one of the criteria,[1] and the orientation of this list was literary rather than conversational.

The Plan

To base a study on conversational conformity, I decided on the following procedure:
1. Assemble approximately 5,000 frequently used idiomatic Spanish expressions.
2. Reduce the number, with help from four competent native speakers, to a more manageable 1,100.

---

[1]See Hayward Keniston, *Spanish Idiom List* (Macmillan, 1939).

3. Alphabetize the expressions, providing an English translation and a vernacular example in Spanish for each.
4. Set up a system of five value levels (0, 1, 2, 3, and 4) to determine acceptability and frequency.
5. Select competent native speakers in as many Spanish-speaking countries as possible to evaluate the 1,100 expressions.
6. Collect and collate the data, listing the expressions according to their respective ratings.
7. Make a final list of 1,000 idioms available to interested persons.

Modus Operandi

The basic inventory of Spanish idiomatic expressions was compiled after consulting several published lists, checking in their entirety two reputable Spanish dictionaries, and then-inserting expressions from my own and others' experience. Nearly 5,000 expressions resulted, each considered relevant for American students of Spanish. Since a list so long was impractical, it was reduced to 1,100 expressions so that a final compilation would result in at least 1,000 valid expressions after applying the reliability factor over regional, country, and dialectical boundaries.

A concentrated effort was made from the outset to avoid vulgar or slang expressions. Only colloquial items of universal and acceptable usage were meant to be included.

The list was mimeographed and distributed to competent native Spanish speakers, to whom I am deeply indebted. A facsimile of page one of the list can be found in Appendix 1.

Distribution of Lists

One of the factors contributing to the reliability of the data was that the checkers were chosen and oriented, in most instances, in their home countries. With but a few exceptions the checkers were native-speaking tutors of the Foreign Service Institute—sponsored classes in United States embassies and consulates in Latin America. These individuals were required by job classification to be well educated. More than half of them reportedly consulted from one to a dozen or more acquaintances before making a final judgment for each of the 1,100 expressions. Completed returns were received from forty-five checkers representing nineteen countries, including Mexico, Central America, the Caribbean, South America, and Spain.[2] Each return appeared to have been completed conscientiously, according to written and verbal directions. The judgment, therefore, of an estimated 100 or more native speakers went into the final compilations.

---

[2]Specifically the countries and regions were Mexico 12 (Mexico City 4, Ciudad Juárez, Guadalajara, Hermosillo, Monterrey, Nuevo Laredo, Tampico, Tijuana, Veracruz); Guatemala and El Salvador 3 each; Argentina, Bolivia, Chile, Colombia, Costa Rica, Ecuador, Honduras, Nicaragua, Panama, Peru, and Venezuela each 2; Cuba, Dominican Republic, Paraguay, Spain, and Uruguay each contributing 1.

Collation

In collating, the points for each expression in the forty-five lists were totaled. Expression number 1, *está bien* or *está bueno*, received 172 points of a possible 180; the lowest-rated expression, number 1,000, received 49. In cases where several expressions resulted in the same point total, their numerical listing within the rating was arbitrary. The point total for each expression can be found in Appendix 2.

Format

Parentheses have four principle functions: (1) to indicate alternatives, such as 131 *estar* (or *quedar*) *entendido que;* (2) to indicate possible but optional expansions, as in 412 *cosa* (*digna*) *de ver;* (3) to indicate prepositions often used but not necessary to the idiom, as in 661 *sin fin* (*de*); (4) to indicate words suggested for expansions beyond the idiom itself, such as 798 *tener detenido* (*algo*). Brackets are used only in instances where an alternative not rated by checkers in the original was thought to be of sufficient importance to be added for the reader's convenience.

Separate listings of both the Spanish idioms and their English equivalents have been included. Each idiom is listed alphabetically with its numerical frequency, by which the reader can find a more complete definition and a usage example.

Definition

Historically the word *idiom* in Latin signified language itself. In English it has come to mean an expression peculiar to itself in grammatical construction, or, to cite from Webster's Collegiate Dictionary, "an expression . . . having a meaning that [as a whole] cannot be derived from the conjoined meanings of its elements."

Since few would be wholly in agreement as to where to draw the line between *idiom* and *vocabulary* it appears desirable to skirt a formal definition of *idiom* for purposes of this work. Instead, I have chosen to list and describe the constituent "types" treated under the general term *idiom* as follows: A large portion of the expressions included belong to the category described in the dictionary definition, such as 106 *poner el grito en el cielo* (to hit the ceiling), in which the lexical makeup is completely different from the meanings of its individual words. Another important group embodies verbal expressions which contain a verb and a preposition, as in 26 *preguntar por* (ask about). A third grouping comprehends certain compound conjunctions, such as 56 *tanto como* (as much as), or compound prepositions, as in 53 *dentro de* (inside of). In addition there are a few other combinations which are idiomatic in their effect but which may not fall into a well-defined grouping, as illustrated by 104 *mejor dicho* (better yet), 632 *todo lo posible* (everything possible), and 502 *largos años* (many years). All have fixed meanings, which learners must gain for themselves in improving their Spanish communication skills.

Conclusion

The data offered herein represent the consensus of many knowledgeable people of the Hispanic world, who have dedicated hundreds of hours of work to their preparation. The thousand Spanish idioms are listed in a descending order of occurrence as judged by their checkers.

Although this was never intended to be an in-depth, erudite study, my hope has always been that the result would be useful to students of Spanish. I make no claim either that the resulting expressions are the only ones commonly used in the language or that their arrangement is in the same order in which a majority of native speakers of the language might place them. I have, however, made a scrupulous effort to accurately report and present the native evaluators' findings, for whatever value they may have.

PART 1
NUMERICAL LISTING ON FREQUENCY OF OCCURRENCE

1   **Está bien** or **está bueno**
¡Está bien, haz lo que quieras!

All right, good, fine, correct, OK

2   **Dar las gracias**
No le dieron las gracias por el favor
que les hizo.

To thank, express gratitude, be
grateful

3   **Pensar en**
¿En qué piensas?

To think of, about or over; intend

4   **Ganarse la vida**
Me gano la vida como puedo.

To earn (or make) a living

5   **De memoria**
Me lo aprendí de memoria.

By heart, from memory

6   **Poner la mesa**
Ya puse la mesa para cenar.

To set the table

7   **Valer la pena**
No vale la pena ir al centro.

To be worth(while), advantageous,
profitable

8   **Tener cuidado**
Tenga cuidado al bajar.

To be careful, watchful, attentive,
on guard

9   **Hay que**
Hay que hacerlo ahora mismo.

It is necessary, obligatory, or
required to (that)

10   **Otra vez**
¿Volverá usted por aquí otra vez?

Again, once more, another time

11   **Ir de compras**
El jueves es un buen día para ir de
compras.

To go shopping, do marketing

12   **Estar de luto**
Estoy de luto porque se murió
mi abuelita.

To be in mourning, bereavement;
manifest sorrow for a death

13   **Dar una vuelta**
Vamos a dar una vuelta por el
parque.

To walk, saunter, take a stroll

14   **Dar el pésame por**
Tienes que darle el pésame a
María por la muerte de su hermano.

To present or give one's
condolences (for, on), extend one's
sympathy (for, on)

15   **A carta cabal**
Es honrado a carta cabal.

Thoroughly, in every respect, fully

16   **Tal vez**
Tal vez mañana podamos vernos.

Perhaps, maybe, possibly, probably,
perchance

17   **Querer decir**
¿Qué quiere decir esta frase?

To mean

18 **Por extenso**   In detail, at great length
El informe fue bien recibido, por
extenso y bien documentado.

19 **Por casualidad**   By chance, by the way, incidentally
¿Por casualidad, lo conoce?

20 **Poco a poco**   Little by little, gradually, progres-
Poco a poco aprenderá usted a   sively, bit by bit, slowly
hablar español.

21 **Estar de moda**   To be popular, fashionable, stylish,
Ese artista está muy de moda.   smart

22 **En punto**   On the dot, sharp, exactly
Debemos llegar a las seis en punto.

23 **Desde hace**   For (a certain time lapse), over a
Lo conozco desde hace muchos   period of, dating from
años.

24 **De nuevo**   Again, once more, another time,
Tendrá que empezarlo de nuevo.   anew

25 **Preocuparse por**   To worry about, be concerned for
No se preocupe usted por eso.   or about

26 **Preguntar por**   To inquire about, ask for (a
Preguntaron por usted esta   person)
mañana.

27 **Por lo menos**   At least, leastwise
Por lo menos costará cien pesos.

28 **Ida y vuelta**   Round-trip, two-way
Por favor deme un boleto de ida
y vuelta a Acapulco.

29 **Hacer cola**   To stand in line, line up, queue
He estado haciendo cola más de   (up)
dos horas.

30 **Ocurrírsele a uno**   To occur to one, cross one's mind
Se me ocurrió una buena idea.

31 **De todas maneras**   At any rate, in any event, no matter
De todas maneras, iremos.   what happens

32 **Hasta la fecha**   Up to now, to date
Hasta la fecha no hemos tenido
noticias de él.

33 **Hacerse tarde**   To become late, be getting
Se hace tarde y no estamos listas.   (or growing) late

34 **Frente a**   In front of
El coche paró frente a la puerta.

Freq.	Spanish	English
35	**Equivocarse de** Me equivoqué de autobús.	To be mistaken or wrong about (something)
36	**Decidirse a** Se decidió a casarse con ella.	To make up one's mind to, decide to, resolve to
37	**De enfrente** Viven en la casa de enfrente.	Across (the street), directly opposite, in front (of)
38	**Alegrarse de** Me alegro mucho de verla.	To be glad or happy about (something)
39	**Acabar de** (+ infinitive) Acabo de llegar de la tienda.	To have just (+ past participle)
40	**Sin querer** Lo hizo sin querer.	Unwittingly, unintentionally
41	**Por lo visto** Por lo visto, no se acordó de que tenía que venir.	Apparently, seemingly, evidently, judging by appearances
42	**Pasar un buen rato** Después de todo, pasamos un buen rato.	To have a good time, enjoy one's self
43	**Parece mentira** Parece mentira que tenga esa edad.	It hardly seems possible, it appears to be impossible
44	**No hay de qué** ¡Muchas gracias! No hay de qué.	Don't mention it, think nothing of it, you're welcome
45	**Lo de menos** Eso es lo de menos. Yo te presto el dinero.	Of little importance, insignificant
46	**La mayor parte (de)** La mayor parte de los asistentes a la fiesta se divertieron mucho.	The majority (of), the bulk (of)
47	**En** (or **de**) **broma** Lo dije en broma.	As a joke, in jest
48	**Hacer caso a** No le hago caso de lo que dice.	To pay attention to, heed, obey
49	**Faltar a** Faltó a la clase el lunes pasado. (2) ¡No le falte a su madre!	To absent one's self from, miss; (2) to show disrespect to
50	**Hacer buenas migas** El perro y el gato no hacen buenas migas.	To get along well together, be congenial

51	**Echar a perder** Ha echado a perder el trabajo.	To spoil, ruin, go to waste
52	**Delante de** No digas esas cosas delante de una señora.	In the presence of, in front of
53	**Dentro de** Está dentro del cajón (2) Vendrá dentro de dos meses.	Inside (of); (2) in or within (a period of time)
54	**Dar que hacer** ¡Estos niños me dan tanto que hacer!	To make or cause (extra) work
55	**Al revés** La historia no es así, precisamente es al revés. (2) Tiene la blusa puesta al revés.	The contrary, opposite; (2) wrong side (inside) out
56	**Tanto como** No creo que usted trabaje tanto como él.	As much as
57	**Por primera vez** Llevé a Juanito al museo por primera vez.	For the first time
58	**Por poco** No miré por donde iba, y por poco me caigo.	Almost, just about, nearly
59	**Por ahora** Por ahora tenemos bastante comida.	For the present, for now
60	**Parecido a** Yo tengo un traje muy parecido al suyo.	Like, similar to
61	**Pagar a plazos** Pagaron el refrigerador a plazos.	To pay in installments, make payments
62	**Oír hablar de** ¿Ha oído usted hablar del nuevo descubrimiento?	To hear about, to hear tell of
63	**Por adelantado**	Beforehand, in advance
64	**Mientras tanto** Volverán pronto, mientras tanto, juguemos una partida de cartas.	Meanwhile, in the meantime
65	**Meterse en lo que no le importa** No te metas en lo que no te importa.	To be (too) inquisitive, intrusive, prying, or nosy; butt in

66	**Estar de acuerdo**	To agree, be of the same opinion
	Estuvieron de acuerdo en todo.	
67	**En lugar de**	Instead of, in place of
	En lugar de comer aquí, vamos a casa.	
68	**En cuanto**	As soon as, the moment that
	En cuanto llegue, avíseme.	
69	**Dejar de** (+ infinitive)	To stop, cease, quit (+ gerund)
	Dejó de comer al entrar José.	
70	**De ahora en adelante**	From now on, in the future
	De ahora en adelante lo haremos así.	
71	**De más**	Too much, too many
	Le dieron seis libras de más.	
72	**Con mucho gusto**	Gladly, willingly, with great pleasure
	Lo haré con mucho gusto.	
73	**Tener la culpa**	To be to blame, be at fault
	Ella tiene la culpa de todo.	
74	**Tener ganas de**	To feel like, desire, wish
	Tengo ganas de pasear.	
75	**Quedarse con**	To take (as in choosing or buying); (2) to remain or stay with
	Me quedo con el azul.	
	(2) Me quedo con mis padres.	
76	**No poder ver ni en pintura**	Not to be able to stand the sight of
	No puedo ver el aceite de ricino ni en pintura.	
77	**Por fuera**	On the outside, on the exterior
	Por fuera la casa es muy bonita.	
78	**Ir del brazo**	To walk arm in arm
	Van del brazo.	
79	**Importarle a uno**	To matter or be of importance to one, concern one
	A él no le importa.	
80	**Hacer falta**	To be necessary; have need of, lack
	Es siempre lo mismo — le hace falta dinero.	
81	**Fijarse en**	To pay attention to, mark one's word
	Fíjese usted en lo que le digo.	
82	**Estar con**	To have (an illness or discomfort)
	Estoy con dolor de cabeza.	

83	**Encargarse de** Me encargaré del trabajo.	To take charge of, assume responsibility for
84	**En vano** Esperé en vano toda la tarde.	In vain, fruitlessly
85	**En el fondo** En el fondo era una buena persona.	At heart, by nature
86	**Detrás de** Detrás de los árboles hay una casa.	Behind, in back of
87	**Dentro de poco** Nos veremos dentro de poco.	Soon, in a little while, shortly
88	**De mal en peor** Vamos de mal en peor.	From bad to worse
89	**En el extranjero** Vivió largos años en el extranjero.	Abroad, out of the country
90	**Tener deseos de** Tengo muchos deseos de verlo.	To want to, be eager to
91	**A propósito** A propósito, ¿has leído tu novela? (2) Sin duda lo hizo a propósito.	By the way; (2) on purpose
92	**Dar lástima** Su estado daba lástima.	To arouse pity or regret
93	**Dar cuerda a** No le di cuerda al reloj anoche.	To wind (a watch, clock, toy)
94	**Todavía** [or **aún**] **no** Todavía no he comido.	Not yet
95	**Darle a uno vergüenza** No me atrevo a decírselo, me da vergüenza.	To be ashamed, to be (too) bashful or shy
96	**Tarde o temprano** Tarde o temprano lo sabrá.	Sooner or later, eventually
97	**Tan pronto como** Tan pronto como lo haga, avíseme.	As soon as, the moment that
98	**Sobre todo** Me gusta el café, sobre todo si está bien caliente.	Especially, particularly, above all
99	**Sin remedio** Es un caso sin remedio.	Hopeless, beyond solution
100	**Por última vez** Por última vez, ¿viene usted?	Finally, for the last time

101	**Pedir prestado** ¿Puedo pedirte prestado el auto para el próximo domingo?	To borrow, ask to lend
102	**Ocuparse de** Se ocupa muy poco de su familia.	To take care of, attend to
103	**No poder ver a alguien** No puedo verlo.	Not to be able to tolerate someone
104	**Mejor dicho** Iré a las tres, mejor dicho, a las tres y cuarto.	Or rather, better yet
105	**Llamar la atención** Le gusta llamar la atención. (2) Le llamé la atención por su falta de respeto.	To attract attention, call attention to; (2) to reprimand, censure, chide
106	**Poner el grito en el cielo** Como lo temíamos, Juana puso el grito en el cielo.	To make a great fuss, agitate, hit the ceiling
107	**Hacerle daño a uno** Me hace daño la comida picante.	To hurt or be harmful to one; not agree (physically) with one
108	**En vez de** Voy a comer pescado en vez de carne.	Instead of, rather than
109	**Frente a frente** Los dos enemigos estaban frente a frente	Face to face
110	**En cambio** Baila mal; en cambio, canta muy bien.	But, on the other hand
111	**Empleársele bien a uno** Perdí mi billetera; pero me lo tengo bien empleado por ser tan descuidado.	To serve someone right, get one's due
112	**De aquí** (or **de hoy**) **en adelante** De aquí en adelante tendremos que gastar menos.	From now on, henceforth
113	**Cuando quiera** Cuando usted quiera, empezamos.	Whenever or as soon as you would like, when you are ready
114	**Al principio** Al principio me parecía fácil el trabajo.	At first, initially, at the outset
115	**Y pico*** Nos cobró doscientos pesos y pico.	And some odd (as in numbers), and something

116 **Y así sucesivamente**   And so on, et cetera
Ponga una capa de arroz, otra de
carne molida sazonada, y así
sucesivamente.

117 **Tomar el pelo**   To deceive, pull one's leg (colloq.)
Creo que me estás tomando el pelo.

118 **Tener razón**   To be right, correct
Si no tienes razón, mejor cállate.

119 **Sin falta**   Without fail
Venga usted sin falta a las once.

120 **Quedar en**   To agree on, come to a mutual
Quedamos en que vendría a las   understanding or decision about
ocho.

121 **Por supuesto**   Of course, certainly
¡Por supuesto que puedes venir!

122 **Por aquí cerca**   Somewhere near here, around here,
¿Hay un buen restaurante por aquí   in the vicinity
cerca?

123 **Ponerse de acuerdo**   To come to an agreement, be in
Después de discutir mucho se   accord
pusieron de acuerdo.

124 **Perderse de vista**   To be lost from sight, vanish,
En pocos minutos el avión se perdió disappear
de vista.

125 **Pensar de**   To think of, have an opinion of or
¿Qué piensas de Juan?   about

126 **Pasar el rato**   To kill time, pass the time away
¿Cómo pasaremos el rato?

127 **Menos de**   Fewer than, less than
Tengo menos de doce años.

128 **Llevarse bien con**   To get along well with
Se lleva muy bien con sus amigos.

129 **Hasta cierto punto**   To a certain point or extent
Hasta cierto punto tiene razón.

130 **Estar rendido**   To be exhausted, all in, depleted
Después de trabajar catorce horas
seguidas, estoy rendido.

*Not acceptable in Chile.

131 **Estar** (or **quedar**) **entendido que**   To be understood or agreed (that)
Está entendido que empezaremos
mañana.

132 **En la mitad** (**de**)   In the middle of
El muchacho se encontró en la
mitad del problema.

133 **En fila**   In (a) line
Los niños estaban formados en fila.

134 **El día menos pensado**   When one least expects
El día menos pensado vienen a
vernos.

135 **Después de**   After, following
Iremos después de comer.

136 **Desde que**   Ever since, from the moment that
La quiero desde que la conocí.

137 **Dejar en paz**   To leave alone, let be
Déjeme en paz porque estoy
durmiendo la siesta.

138 **A más tardar**   At the latest
A más tardar, llegará esta noche.

139 **Por fin**   At last, finally
Por fin pude encontrarlo.

140 **No ser ni la sombra de uno**   To be but a shadow of one's former
Era muy bella, y ahora no es ni la   self
sombra de lo que fue.

141 **Poco después** (**de**)   Soon after, a little after
Me casé poco después de que
terminó la guerra.

142 **Limitar con**   To be bounded or bordered by;
México limita al norte con los   (2) to be held down or back
Estados Unidos de Norteamérica.
(2) El jefe me limita con su actitud.

143 **Hecho y derecho**   Mature, grown-up, full-fledged
Es un hombre hecho y derecho.

144 **En resumidas cuentas**   In short, in a word
En resumidas cuentas, no quise
venir.

145 **En representación de**   As an emissary of, representing
Fue a Chile en representación de
su país.

146   **Desde entonces**   Since then, since that time
      Desde entonces he cambiado mucho.

147   **De repente**   All of a sudden, unexpectedly
      Llegó de repente a la casa.

148   **De ninguna manera**   By no means, under no circum-
      De ninguna manera lo aceptaré.   stances

149   **De la noche a la mañana**   Overnight, all at once
      Se hizo rico de la noche a la mañana.

150   **Costar mucho trabajo**   To be difficult, hard
      Me costó mucho trabajo arreglar
      el asunto.

151   **Dar rabia**   To anger, make furious
      Me da rabia no haber ido.

152   **Darse cuenta de**   To realize, be aware of
      Se dio cuenta de su error.

153   **Confiar en**   To rely on, trust in, count on
      Usted puede confiar en él.

154   **Dar la vuelta a algo**   To turn or rotate something;
      Hay que darle dos vueltas a la llave.   (2) to go around something
      (2) Dimos la vuelta a la manzana.

155   **Dar mucha pena**   To make one sorry, be
      Me da mucha pena verlo así.   disconcerting

156   **Al por mayor**   Wholesale, in large quantity
      Vendía sólo al por mayor.

157   **Al fin**   At last, finally
      Al fin se quedaron solos.

158   **Al contrario**   On the other hand, on the contrary
      ¿Ha dicho eso?
      Al contrario, no lo ha dicho.

159   **A última hora**   At the last moment, in the nick of
      A última hora todo se solucionó.   time

160   **A duras penas**   With great difficulty
      A duras penas estamos haciendo
      frente a la situación.

161   **Ver visiones**   To see things, have false notions
      ¡Está usted viendo visiones!

162   **Rendir cuentas a** (or **ante**)   To give or render an accounting to
      Tuvo que rendir cuentas a su
      padre.

163   **Por si acaso**
Por si acaso lo necesita, lleve usted
dinero.

Just in case, if by chance, in the
event that

164   **Por ningún motivo**
No se comprometa a firmar el
documento por ningún motivo.

Under no circumstances, no matter
what

165   **Por las nubes**
¡Los precios están por las nubes!

Sky-high, extreme, lofty (in price
or praise)

166   **Por eso**
Por eso quiero salir temprano.

For that reason, so, therefore

167   **¿Por dónde?**
¿Por dónde está la salida?

Which way? Where?

168   **Por dentro**
La caja está pintada por dentro.

Inside, on the inside, within

169   **Recomendar algo a uno**
Me recomendó que llegara
temprano. (2) Le recomiendo a
usted mi perrito por una semana.

To make a special request of someone for something; (2) to charge a
person with something, entrust
something to someone

170   **Plan de estudios**
Han cambiado el plan de estudios
en la universidad.

Curriculum, set of courses

171   **Pasado de moda**
Este vestido está pasado de moda.

Out of date, out of style, passé

172   **Pagar los gastos**
Juan va a ir a Europa en viaje de
estudios, y la compañía donde
trabaja va a pagar los gastos.

To pay the expenses, foot the bill,
stand the cost

173   **Hacer caso de**
No hagas caso de lo que te cuente.

To pay attention to, take into
account, respect, esteem

174   **Es decir**
Es decir, estamos a punto de
romper nuestro compromiso.

That is to say, that is, in other
words, specifically

175   **Entusiasmarse con**
Los muchachos se entusiasmaron
con la música.

To be enthusiastic about, be
eagerly attentive to

176   **En voz alta** or **en voz baja**
No hable usted en voz tan baja, no
le oigo.

Out loud; in a soft voice

177   **Echar de menos**
Echa de menos a sus amigos.

To miss, feel the lack or loss of,
long for

178   **Digno de confianza**   Reliable, trustworthy, reputable
      Es una persona digna de confianza.

179   **De lo lindo**   Very much, greatly, wonderfully
      Gozamos de lo lindo en la fiesta.

180   **De buena fe** or **de mala fe**   In good faith, with complete
      Lo hizo de buena fe.   confidence; with no confidence

181   **De acuerdo con**   In accordance, conformity or
      Lo hice de acuerdo con sus   agreement with
      instrucciones.

182   **Dar disgustos a**   To cause distress or grief to
      Ese muchacho le dio muchos
      disgustos a sus padres.

183   **Correr riesgo**   To chance, run risk
      Corrió un gran riesgo.

184   **Contar con**   To depend upon, count on
      Cuento con su ayuda.

185   **A medio hacer**   Half done, incomplete
      Esta trabajo está a medio hacer.

186   **A mano**   By hand; (2) nearby, within reach;
      La carta estaba escrita a mano.   (3) (to be) even
      (2) Póngalo usted a mano.
      (3) Estamos a mano.

187   **A lo mejor**   As luck may have it, like as not
      A lo mejor mañana llueve.

188   **Gracias a**   Thanks to
      Gracias a usted llegué a tiempo.

189   **Sentir en el alma**   To regret deeply, be terribly sorry
      Lo siento en el alma pero no puedo
      ir a tu boda.

190   **Referirse a**   To refer to, have reference to
      ¿A qué se refiere usted al decir eso?

191   **Quitarse un peso de encima**   To take a load off one's mind, be
      Me confesó sus faltas porque quería   relieved
      quitarse un peso de encima.

192   **Por un lado... por otro**   On the one side (or hand) . . . on the
      Por un lado me gusta; pero por   other, in a way . . . in another way
      otro no.

193   **Por otra parte**   On the other hand
      Por otra parte, el gobierno ha
      decidido colaborar también.

194   **Por ningún lado** [or **ninguna parte**]   Nowhere, not any place
      No lo encontré por ningún lado.

195	**Ponerse de pie** Cuando entró el presidente se pusieron todos de pie.	To get up, stand, arise
196	**Ir a medias** Iremos a medias en el negocio.	To go fifty-fifty, go halves
197	**Hacerse el tonto** No te hagas el tonto, que te conozco.	To play dumb, act the fool
198	**Extrañarle a uno** Me extraña que no haya llegado aún.	To seem strange to one
199	**De pura casualidad** Me encontré con él de pura casualidad.	Purely by chance
200	**Estar muy metido en** Juan está muy metido en política.	To be deeply involved in
201	**Estar en las nubes** Siempre está en las nubes.	To daydream, muse
202	**Estar a cargo** ¿Quién está a cargo de la sección de embarques?	To be in charge
203	**En primer lugar** En primer lugar tengo que hacer este trabajo.	In the first place
204	**Desde lejos** Desde lejos le reconocimos.	From a distance, from afar
205	**De esta manera** (or **este modo**) Hágalo usted de esta manera.	This way, in this manner
206	**Darle a uno lo mismo** Todo le da lo mismo.	To be all the same to one
207	**Dar facilidades** El gobierno nos dio toda clase de facilidades para la investigación.	To facilitate, offer every assistance
208	**Con tal que** Vendrá con tal que no llueva.	Provided that, in the event that
209	**Con tiempo** Avíseme con tiempo.	In (good) time, beforehand, in advance
210	**Ahora mismo** Hágalo ahora mismo. (2) Salió ahora mismo.	At once, right away; (2) just, just now
211	**Todas las veces que** Todas las veces que lo veo me pregunta por usted.	Whenever, every time

212   **Tener lugar**   To take place, be held, occur
      La ceremonia tuvo lugar en el
      cementerio.

213   **Tener fe en**   To believe or have faith in
      Tengo mucha fe en él.

214   **Sin embargo**   However, nevertheless
      Aunque es el estado más pequeño,
      es, sin embargo, el más poblado.

215   **Punto de vista**   Point of view, standpoint
      Díganos cuál es su punto de vista.

216   **Por la mitad**   In half, in the middle
      Parta usted esto por la mitad.

217   **Ponerse a**   To begin to, start out to
      De repente se puso a correr.

218   **Pasar por alto**   To overlook, forget, gloss or pass
      Hemos pasado por alto muchos   over
      puntos importantes.

219   **Darle a uno la gana**   To feel like, want to
      ¿Por qué lo hace? Porque me da
      la gana.

220   **No hay más remedio que**   There's nothing to do but
      No hay más remedio que dejarlo
      marchar.

221   **Negarse a**   To refuse to, decline to
      Se negó a ayudarme.

222   **Nada de particular**   Nothing special, nothing unusual
      Esa casa no tiene nada de particular.

223   **Llevar puesto**   To wear or be wearing (clothes or
      Lleva puestos los aretes que le   jewelry)
      regalaron el día de su cumpleaños.

224   **Lejos de**   Far from, far removed from, distant
      Vive demasiado lejos de la ciudad.   from

225   **Hacer buen papel** or **hacer mal**   To make a good showing; to make
      papel   a poor showing
      Argentina hizo un buen papel
      en el Mundial.

226   **Desde un principio**   Right from the start or beginning
      Desde un principio me pareció
      que estaba equivocado.

227   **En la actualidad**   At the present time, right now
      En la actualidad escasea el arroz.

228 **Hasta aquí**   So far, up to now
Hasta aquí todo está bien.

229 **De lo contrario**   Otherwise, if not
Saldré a las seis; de lo contrario
llegaré tarde.

230 **De etiqueta**   Formal, full dress
Habrá un baile de etiqueta en el
Casino.

231 **Dar una mano**   To apply (a coat of paint, varnish,
Déle una mano de pintura al cuarto.   etc.); (2) to help out, lend a hand
(2) Démosle una mano ahora que
nos necesita.

232 **Boca abajo** or **boca arriba**   Face down, on one's stomach; face
El niño duerme boca abajo.   upward, on one's back

233 **Dar un paseo**   To take a walk or stroll
¿Le gustaría dar un paseo por el
parque?

234 **Alguna vez**   Sometimes, now and then, every so
Alguna vez voy a comer al   often
restaurante.

235 **A mediados de**   About or around the middle of (a
Estamos a mediados de mes.   time period, e.g., week, month)

236 **A fines de**   Toward the end of, late in (a time
A fines de semana volveré a mi casa.   period, e.g., the week, the month)

237 **Abierto de par en par**   Wide open
La puerta estaba abierta de par en
par.

238 **A cambio de**   In exchange or trade for
Le daré este libro a cambio de ese otro.

239 **Buen genio** or **mal genio**   Good nature or temper; bad
Es una persona de buen genio.   disposition or temper

240 **Tomar medidas**   To take measurements; (2) to take
Me tomaron medidas para el traje.   measures or steps
(2) Tomaron medidas para evitar
la rebelión.

241 **Tocarle a uno**   To be one's turn; (2) to concern
Le toca jugar. (2) Fue un asunto   one
que me toca de cerca.

242 **Ser aficionado a**   To be a fan or avid follower of
Soy un gran aficionado al béisbol.

243 **Salir ganando**   To come out ahead, win
¿Quién salió ganando?

244 **Saber lo que es bueno**   To know what one is missing, know
Si no has visto esa película, no   what is going on, be with it (colloq.)
sabes lo que es bueno.

245 **Responder por**   To be responsible for or vouch for
¿Quién responde por él?   (a person)

246 **Por más que**   However much, no matter how
Por más que llame usted, nadie   much
contestará.

247 **Por las buenas**   Willingly, of one's own accord
Me lo dio por las buenas.

248 **No dar el brazo a torcer**   To be stubborn, unyielding
Nunca da su brazo a torcer, aunque
esté equivocado.

249 **Ni siquiera**   Not even, not a single
No dijo ni siquiera una palabra.

250 **Mientras no**   Unless, if . . . not
Mientras no estudie usted no
aprenderá.

251 **Mientras más... más** or **mientras**   The more . . . the more; (2) the
menos... menos   less . . . the less
Mientras más duermo, más ganas
tengo de trabajar. (2) Mientras
menos trabajes, menos dinero
tendrás disponible.

252 **Merecer la pena**   To be worthwhile
No merece la pena que te pongas
a llorar por una tontería.

253 **Más allá (de)**   Farther on, beyond
El pueblo está más allá de aquellos
árboles.

254 **Hacerse ilusiones**   To deceive or fool one's self
No nos hagamos ilusiones con ese
proyecto.

255 **Formar parte de**   To be a member or part of
Formó parte de la sección
administrativa.

256 **Hacerse el sordo**   To refuse to consider, turn a deaf
Se hizo el sordo a mis peticiones.   ear

257 **Estar prevenido**   To be ready, prepared, forewarned
Como estaba prevenido, no lo
sorprendieron.

258 Estar de turno
El policía estaba de turno aquella
noche.

To be on duty

259 Enterarse de
Acabo de enterarme de la mala
noticia de la muerte de su padre.

To find out or learn about, become
aware of

260 En un dos por tres
En un dos por tres lo arregló todo.

In a jiffy, quickly

261 Echarse a (reír, llorar, etc.)
Al oír el chiste se echó a reír.

To begin, burst out, suddenly start
to (laugh, cry, etc.)

262 En mangas de camisa
Por el calor estaban en mangas de
camisa.

In shirt sleeves

263 En presencia de
Lo dijo en presencia de todos.

In front of, before

264 Advertir algo a alguien
Ya se lo advertí a usted.

To tell one (so)

265 De modo que
¿De modo que es usted americano?
(2) Arreglé las cosas de modo que
usted pudiera venir.

So, and so; (2) so that

266 Dejar dicho
Dejó dicho que vendría a las cuatro.

To leave word

267 Echar la culpa a
No me eches la culpa a mí.

To lay the blame on

268 Dar parte
Dieron parte del robo a la policía.

To inform, notify, report

269 Dar la razón
Le doy la razón.

To agree (with), acknowledge (a
person) to be right

270 ¡Buen provecho!
(customary greeting before or after
a meal)

Good appetite! Enjoy your meal!
May you profit from your food!

271 A pesar de
A pesar de todo, lo haremos.

In spite of, despite

272 Tomar nota de
Tomé nota de todo lo que había
ocurrido en el viaje.

To take note of, jot down

273 Todo lo contrario
No es lo que usted dice, sino todo
lo contrario.

Just the opposite, the other way
around

274 Tener fama de
Tiene fama de sabio.

To have the reputation of

275	**Tener en la punta de la lengua** Tengo su apellido en la punta de la lengua, y no puedo recordarlo.	To have on the tip of one's tongue
276	**Tener en cuenta** Tenga en cuenta lo que le digo.	To keep in mind, consider
277	**Prestar atención** Se ruega prestar atención.	To pay attention, be alert
278	**Pesarle a uno** No me pesa haberlo dicho.	To regret, be sorry for
279	**Perder la cabeza** Nunca pierde la cabeza a pesar de tener mucho dinero.	To lose one's head, lose one's cool (colloq.)
280	**Hacerse rogar** Le gusta hacerse rogar.	To be coaxed, importuned
281	**Meterse con** ¿Por qué se mete usted conmigo?	To pick a fight with
282	**Hacer un mandado** María quiere que le haga un mandado a medio día.	To run an errand
283	**Hacer juego** Ese sombrero hace juego con el traje.	To match, go well (with)
284	**Hablar hasta por los codos** Ese muchacho habla hasta por los codos.	To chatter, talk idly
285	**Estar de viaje** Estuvimos de viaje durante el verano.	To be traveling, be on the road
286	**Estar a punto de** Estábamos a punto de salir cuando llegaron.	To be at the point of, be about to
287	**Desde ahora** Desde ahora voy a venir todos los días.	From now on, beginning now
288	**De un día para otro** De un día para otro el enfermo se agravó.	From one day to the next, day by day
289	**De buena gana** or **de mala gana** Hizo el trabajo de buena gana.	Willingly, with pleasure; unwill- ingly, reluctantly
290	**Correr por cuenta de uno** Eso corre por mi cuenta.	To be one's affair, be up to one
291	**Convenirle a uno** No me conviene aceptar eso.	To be to one's advantage, be advisable

292 **Con permiso**   If you don't mind, with your
     Con su permiso, se hace tarde.   permission, please excuse me

293 **Burlarse de**   To make fun of, poke fun at, jest
     Se burla de todo el mundo.

294 **Algo por el estilo**   Something like that, something
     ¿Por qué no le ragalas una   of the kind
     muñeca, o algo por el estilo?

295 **Además de**   In addition to
     Además de fruta vamos a tomar
     helado.

296 **A lo lejos**   In the distance, at a distance, way
     A lo lejos vimos unas casas.   over there

297 **Estar a gusto**   To be comfortable, at ease,
     ¿Está usted a gusto?   contented, as one likes it

298 **Todo lo demás**   Everything else
     Dame el diccionario, y quédate con
     todo lo demás.

299 **Salirse con la suya**   To have or get one's own way
     Siempre se sale con la suya.

300 **Por lo general**   Usually, in general, ordinarily
     ¿Qué bebe usted por lo general,
     vino o cerveza?

301 **Ponerse colorado**   To blush
     Al oírlo se puso colorada.

302 **Poner en ridículo**   To make a fool of, humiliate
     La conducta de su mujer lo puso en
     ridículo.

303 **Librarse de**   To get rid of, escape from, avoid
     Al fin nos libramos de él.

304 **Hacer gracia**   To strike one (as) funny
     Me hace gracia lo que dice.

305 **Estar de malas**   To be out of luck, hapless
     Estamos de malas; no hemos
     podido pescar nada hoy.

306 **En fin**   In short; (2) well (expletive)
     En fin, ella no lo quería.
     (2) En fin, ya veremos.

307 **Echar al correo**   To mail, post (letters, etc.)
     ¿Echó usted las cartas al correo?

308   **Disculparse por**   To apologize for
Tengo que disculparme por lo
tarde que llegué.

309   **Constarle a uno**   To be evident to one
Me consta que no salió ayer.

310   **Acerca de**   About, concerning, with reference
No sé nada acerca de eso.   or regard to, having to do with

311   **Venir a parar**   To turn out, end up
¿En qué vino a parar ese asunto?

312   **Tomar a broma**   To take lightly or as a joke
Todo lo toma a broma.

313   **Ponerse en contra de**   To oppose, be against
La mayoría de los diputados se
pusieron en contra del proyecto.

314   **No tener pelos en la lengua**   To be outspoken, unreserved in
Esa muchacha no tiene pelos en la   speech
lengua para decir lo que siente.

315   **No tener remedio**   To be beyond repair, help, or
Desgraciadamente, no tiene remedio.   recourse

316   **No ser cosa de juego**   Not to be a laughing matter
Ten mucho cuidado, que no es cosa
de juego.

317   **Molestarse en**   To bother about, take the trouble
No se moleste en hacer tantos   to
viajes.

318   **Informarse de**   To find out about, gather
¿Se ha informado usted de lo que   information on
necesita para entrar en el país?

319   **A que...**   I'll bet . . .
A que no adivina usted lo que me
ha ocurrido hoy.

320   **Estar de sobra**   To be in the way, be superfluous
Yo aquí estoy de sobra.

321   **De pronto**   Abruptly, all of a sudden
De pronto apareció.

322   **De ningún modo**   By no (any) means, under no (any)
No iré de ningún modo.   circumstances

323   **Darse prisa**   To hurry, move quickly
¡Dése prisa, que perdemos el tren!

324   **Compadecerse de alguien** (or **algo**)   To pity, sympathize with, feel sorry
No quieren compadecerse del   for someone (or something)
desgraciado.

325	**Aprovechar la ocasión** Ahora que todo está en silencio, vamos a aprovechar la ocasión para leer a gusto.	To take advantage of the situation
326	**A menudo** Iba a verlo a menudo.	Often, frequently
327	**A la vez** Todos querían hablar a la vez.	At once, simultaneously
328	**Ya lo creo** —¿Quiere usted venir? —¡Ya lo creo!	Of course, certainly
329	**Tropezar con** Tropecé con él en la calle.	To run onto, encounter, come or stumble upon
330	**Tomar a pecho** No lo tome usted a pecho.	To take seriously or to heart
331	**Suceda lo que suceda** Suceda lo que suceda, yo estaré aquí.	Come what may, no matter what
332	**Quedar bien** [or **mal**] **con** Está quedando bien con ella.	To make [or not make] a hit with, get along [or not get along] with
333	**Prender fuego a** Prendieron fuego a los bosques.	To set on fire
334	**Por las buenas o por las malas** Lo harás por las buenas o por las malas.	Whether one likes it or not
335	**No sea que** Tenemos que darnos prisa no sea que cierren la tienda.	Or else, lest
336	**No poder con** No puedo con él. Es un niño problemático.	Not to be able to stand, endure, control, manage
337	**Fiar(se) en, a,** or **de** Tome usted las precauciones necesarias y no se fíe de lo que José le diga.	To rely on, trust in, count on
338	**Estar en un error** Dispénseme, pero está usted en un error.	To be mistaken, wrong
339	**En lo alto de** La casa está en lo alto de la colina.	On top of
340	**Estar con ánimo de** No estoy con ánimo de ir a la fiesta.	To have a mind or notion to

341   **En tal caso**   In such a case or instance
      En tal caso, avise a su familia.

342   **Estar en deuda con**   To be indebted or obliged to
      Estoy en deuda con usted.

343   **En favor**   In or on behalf (of)
      Fue el único que habló en su favor.

344   **Disponer de**   To spend, squander; (2) to have at
      Dispuso de todo el dinero que le   one's disposal
      di. (2) Dispongo de muy poco
      tiempo.

345   **En efecto**   In fact, right
      ¡En efecto, no sabe nada!

346   **Dirigir la palabra**   To address, speak
      No me dirigió la palabra en varios
      días.

347   **¿De dónde?**   How? Whence? By what means?
      ¿De dónde va a saberlo si nadie se
      lo ha dicho?

348   **Dar a entender**   To pretend; (2) to insinuate, drive
      El da a entender que no le interesa.   at
      (2) ¿Qué quiere dar a entender?

349   **Correr peligro**   To run a risk
      Corrió peligro de perder todo su
      dinero.

350   **Contentarse con**   To be satisfied or happy with
      No se contenta con nada.

351   **Al pie de la letra**   Word for word, thoroughly
      Sabe el asunto al pie de la letra.

352   **Unos cuantos**   Some, a few
      Déme unos cuantos caramelos,
      señorita.

353   **Sudar la gota gorda**   To have a bad time, sweat blood
      Para obtener la visa tuvimos que
      sudar la gota gorda.

354   **Refrescar la memoria**   To refresh one's memory
      Para refrescarte la memoria, te
      diré que en ese año todavía
      estábamos en los Estados Unidos.

355   **Por encima de**   Above, over
      El avión volaba por encima de las
      nubes.

356   **Poner en claro**
Tenemos que poner en claro este lío.

To clear up, unravel

357   **Poner a uno al corriente** (**de**)
Le puse al corriente de lo que
había sucedido.

To inform one, tell one, bring one
up to date

358   **Perder de vista**
Al volver la esquina, lo perdimos
de vista.

To lose sight of

359   **¡Manos a la obra!**
Dejen de perder el tiempo.
¡Manos a la obra!

Let's get to work!

360   **Lo indicado**
Haga usted lo indicado en el
prospecto.

That which is stated, directed, or
requested

361   **Irle a uno bien** [or **mal**]
Ese color le va muy bien.

To be becoming [or unbecoming]

362   **Ganar tiempo**
Vamos a tomar el camino más
corto para ganar tiempo.

To save time

363   **Estarse muriendo por**
Me estoy muriendo por verla.

To be dying to, be anxious to

364   **Esforzarse en, por,** or **para**
Juan continúa esforzándose por
mejorar su situación actual.

To strive to

365   **En cuanto a**
En cuanto a lo que dijo, es mejor
no hacer caso.

Regarding, having to do with

366   **Dar que decir** (or **hablar**)
Eso dará mucho que decir.

To cause criticism

367   **Dar en**
Le dio en la cara con la pelota.
(2) Dio en coleccionar sellos.

To hit; (2) to take to

368   **Dar a luz**
Lucía dio a luz un lindo bebé.

To give birth (to)

369   **Con destino a**
Salió con destino a Buenos Aires.

Bound for, going to

370   **Aquí mismo**
Nos encontraremos aquí mismo.

Right here

371   **Valerse de**
Se valió de muchos medios.

To make use of, avail one's self of

372   **Tocar de oído**   To play by ear
El nunca ha estudiado música;
pero toca de oído bastante bien.

373   **Tener confianza con**   To be on intimate terms with
No tengo suficiente confianza con
él para eso.

374   **Tener la intención de**   To intend or mean to
Tenía la intención de decírselo
pero se me olvidó.

375   **Tener al corriente (de)**   To keep someone posted or
Lo tendré al corriente de lo que   informed (about)
pase.

376   **Saber de sobra**   To be fully aware
Lo sabe usted de sobra.

377   **Prevenirse contra**   To take precautions against
Hay que prevenirse contra las
enfermedades.

378   **Por regla general**   As a general rule, usually
Por regla general no trabajamos
los sábados.

379   **Ponérsele a uno carne de gallina**   To get gooseflesh
Con este frío se me pone la carne
de gallina.

380   **Poner en marcha**   To start, put in motion
No podía poner en marcha el
motor.

381   **Perder la vista**   To go blind, lose one's vision
Si sigue leyendo tanto va a perder
la vista.

382   **Perder el hilo de**   To lose the thread of
No me interrumpas porque pierdo
el hilo de mis pensamientos.

383   **Pasársele a uno**   To get over (a state of mind);
Se enfadó, pero se le pasó pronto.   (2) to forget (to)
(2) Se me pasó cerrar la puerta.

384   **Negocio redondo**   Good or sound bargain
Esa compra fue un negocio redondo.

385   **Llevar ventaja**   To be ahead, have a lead
No creo que pueda alcanzarlos,
le llevan mucha ventaja.

386   **Lado flaco**   Weak side or spot
Conozco muy bien su lado flaco.

387 **Ilusionarse con**   To get excited about, get up one's
     Se ilusiona con cualquier cosa.   hopes about

388 **Hoy en día** or **hoy día**   These days, nowadays
     Hoy en día es muy difícil encontrar
     eso.

389 **Hacerse de noche**   To get dark
     Tengo que irme porque se hace
     de noche.

390 **Hacer frente a**   To face up to, confront
     Había que hacer frente a aquel
     conflicto.

391 **Hacer escala**   To land, make a stop
     El avión hará escala en Bogotá
     y Lima.

392 **En un abrir y cerrar de ojos**   In a very short time, in the
     En un abrir y cerrar de ojos, se   twinkling of an eye
     comió todos los dulces.

393 **En lo futuro**   In or for the future, hereafter
     Procure usted en lo futuro venir
     puntualmente a la oficina.

394 **Echarse atrás**   To back out, withdraw
     Cuento con usted, no se vaya a
     echar atrás.

395 **Cuanto antes**   As soon as possible
     Venga cuanto antes.

396 **Consistir en**   To be a question or matter of
     La felicidad consiste en la
     moderación.

397 **Al derecho**   Right side out
     Fíjese que esté al derecho.

398 **A la moda**   Fashionable, in style
     Siempre lleva trajes a la moda.

399 **A conciencia**   Conscientiously, painstakingly
     Hizo su trabajo a conciencia.

400 **Tener antipatía**   To dislike (someone), have an
     Me tiene antipatía.   aversion (for someone)

401 **Ser de lamentar**   To be regrettable, distressing, too
     Es de lamentar que ocurra esto.   bad

402 **Relacionarse con**   To have dealings with
     No se relacione con tales personas.

403 **Un no sé qué**   A certain something
     Ella tiene un no sé qué que atrae.

404	**No saber dónde meterse** Está tan apenado que no sabe dónde meterse.	Not to know which way to turn
405	**Matar el tiempo** Mató el tiempo leyendo los dibujos animados.	To kill or waste time
406	**No cabe duda (de que)** No cabe duda de que es inglés.	There's no doubt or uncertainty (that)
407	**Matar dos pájaros de** [or **en**] **un tiro** Antes de ir a las tiendas voy a pasar al banco; así mato dos pájaros de un tiro.	To kill two birds with one stone
408	**Más bien** Venga más bien a las siete.	Rather, preferably
409	**Ir al grano** ¡Vamos al grano!	To get to the point
410	**Estrechar la mano (a)** Amigablemente se estrecharon la mano.	To shake hands (with)
411	**En regla** El pasaporte estaba en regla.	In order
412	**Cosa (digna) de ver** El ballet folklórico es cosa digna de ver.	Something worthwhile or worth seeing
413	**Desde luego** ¡Desde luego ustedes vendrán con nosotros!	Of course, naturally
414	**Dejarse de cuentos** Dime la verdad, y déjate de cuentos.	To come to the point, stop beating around the bush
415	**Desde abajo** Desde abajo la casa parecía muy alta.	From below
416	**Dejarle a uno plantado** Me dejó plantada en la esquina.	(1) To leave one in the lurch, leave one high and dry; (2) to stand someone up
417	**De paso** El tío de Jaime no va a quedarse aquí; sólo está de paso. (2) Aludió a la situación solamente de paso.	In transit; (2) in passing
418	**De lado** Hay que poner el piano de lado para que entre.	Sideways, on its side

419   **Comunicarse con**   To get in touch with
      Comuníquese conmigo.

420   **Hay gato encerrado**   There is more than meets the eye
      Se rehusa dar una explicación,
      seguramente es porque hay gato
      encerrado.

421   **Por hoy**   For the present
      Por hoy lo dejaremos pasar.

422   **Hecho a la medida**   Made to order or measure,
      El traje está hecho a la medida.   custom-made

423   **A la carrera**   On the run, hastily, hurriedly
      Lo escribió a la carrera.

424   **A la fuerza**   By force, forcibly
      Habrá que hacerlo a la fuerza.

425   **A escondidas de**   Without the knowledge of
      Los niños llevaron el perro al
      parque a escondidas de su mamá.

426   **Tener presente**   To bear or keep in mind
      Tengo presente lo que me dijo.

427   **Sin parar**   Without a break, endlessly
      A Carmen le encanta trabajar
      sin parar.

428   **Serle a uno igual**   To be all the same to one
      Que venga o no venga me es igual.

429   **Sentirse molesto**   To be annoyed, bothered
      No tenía por qué sentirse molesto.

430   **Por término medio**   On the average
      Por término medio voy al cine una
      vez por semana.

431   **Sacar en claro**   To clear up, come to a conclusion
      No sacó nada en claro.

432   **Rodearse de**   To surround one's self with
      Procuró rodearse de buenos amigos.

433   **Prestarse a**   To lend itself to; (2) to offer to
      Lo que dijo se prestaba a malas
      interpretaciones. (2) Se prestó a
      ayudarnos.

434   **Por lo pronto**   For the time being, in the meantime
      Por lo pronto trabaje usted en
      esto.

435	**Por detrás** El enemigo atacó por detrás. (2) Por detrás hablaba mal de él.	From behind; (2) behind one's back
436	**Pasar revista a** El general va a pasar revista a los soldados.	To review, go over carefully
437	**Participar de** Participaremos de las ganancias.	To share (in)
438	**Oponer resistencia** En el último momento el ejército no opuso resistencia.	To offer resistance
439	**Observar buena conducta** Durante el tiempo que estuvo aquí, observó buena conducta.	To behave well
440	**No hay que darle vueltas** Sólo hay una solución, no hay que darle vueltas al asunto.	There are no two ways about it
441	**¡No hay pero que valga!** ¡Haz lo que te ordeno! ¡No hay pero que valga!	No buts about it!
442	**Jugarse el todo por el todo** Se están jugando el todo por el todo.	To bet everything
443	**Hacer de cuenta (que)** Haga de cuenta que nada ha ocurrido.	To pretend (that), act as if
444	**Estar en vísperas de** Estaba en vísperas de embarcar para Europa.	To be on the eve of, be about to
445	**Estar en vigor** La ley todavía no está en vigor.	To be in effect, in force
446	**Enorgullecerse de** Me enorgullece saber que has tenido éxito en tus actividades, hijo mío.	To pride one's self on boast of
447	**En observación** Estaba en observación en un sanatorio.	Under observation
448	**En lo posible** Procura ayudarlo en lo posible.	As far or as much as possible
449	**En cierta manera** (or **forma**) En cierta manera, tiene usted razón.	In a way

450	**En calidad de** Fue al congreso en calidad de intérprete.	In the capacity of, as
451	**Juntarse con** María ya no se junta con nosotros.	To associate with
452	**Constar de** La obra consta de treinta capítulos.	To be composed of, consist of
453	**Con intención** Lo hizo con intención de molestar a Juan.	Deliberately, knowingly
454	**Como una fiera** Se puso como una fiera.	Like a wild beast, furious(ly)
455	**Cerca de** La estación está cerca del hotel. (2) Son cerca de las once.	Near (location); (2) nearly, about, almost
456	**Ascender a** ¿A cuánto asciende mi deuda? (2) Juan fue ascendido a coronel.	To amount to (in money); (2) to be promoted to
457	**Acusar recibo de** Acusamos recibo de su carta fechada el 10 del mes en curso.	To acknowledge receipt of
458	**A mi** (or **tu, su,** etc.) **modo** Yo hago las cosas a mi modo.	In my (or your, etc.) own way
459	**Tomarse la libertad de** Juan se tomó la libertad de usar el auto de José durante su ausencia.	To take the liberty to
460	**Tener sin cuidado** Me dijo que a ella la tenía sin cuidado.	To care less, care not at all
461	**Tener prisa** Tenía tanta prisa que se le olvidó el sombrero.	To be in a hurry
462	**Sin novedad** Por aquí, estamos sin novedad.	As usual; nothing new, no news
463	**Ser bien** (or **mal**) **recibido** Fue mal recibida su opinión.	To be (or not be) well taken or received
464	**Según parece** Según parece, lloverá toda la tarde.	As it seems, apparently
465	**Saber en qué se queda** ¿Se puede saber en qué quedamos?	To find out where one stands

466 **Ni mucho menos**
No es tonto, ni mucho menos.

Far from it, nor anything like it

467 **Llevar la delantera**
Nos llevan la delantera.

To be ahead, have the lead

468 **Llegar a suceder**
Si eso llega a suceder me alegraré
mucho.

To come to pass, happen

469 **Hacer algo a medias**
No haga usted las cosas a medias.

To do something poorly, do a
halfway job

470 **Estar a la expectativa de**
Juan está a la expectativa de una
buena oportunidad para invertir
sus ahorros.

To be on the lookout for, be
expecting

471 **Desde fuera**
Desde fuera no se ve la casa.

From the outside

472 **De manera que**
Ayer no fui, de manera que tengo
que ir hoy.

So that, as a result

473 **De cuando en cuando**
Vendré a verle de cuando en
cuando.

From time to time, occasionally

474 **Dar ánimo**
Le dio ánimo porque estaba
decaído.

To cheer up, buoy up

475 **A fondo**
Era necesario estudiar el asunto
a fondo.

Thoroughly, fully

476 **Dicho y hecho**
Y dicho y hecho, las cosas resultaron
como habíamos pensado.

No sooner said than done

477 **Abrirle los ojos a uno**
La experiencia sufrida le abrió los
ojos.

To open someone's eyes; disabuse
someone

478 **Tener relación con**
Eso no tiene ninguna relación con
el asunto que estamos tratando.

To have connection with, have
relation to

479 **Sin ton ni son**
Habla sin ton ni son.

Without rhyme or reason

480 **Seguir los pasos a**
La policía le sigue los pasos al
ladrón.

To keep an eye on, to check

481	**Tener gracia** Eso sí que tiene gracia.	To be funny, witty
482	**Saber a** La sopa sabe a ajo.	To have the flavor of, taste like
483	**Quedar en** or **de** Quedamos en llegar el domingo.	To agree to, promise to
484	**Punto por punto** Lo contó todo punto por punto.	Step by step, in detail
485	**Presumir de** Presume de elegante.	To think of one's self as, consider one's self to be
486	**Preguntarse si, cuándo, cómo,** etc. Me pregunto cuándo volverá.	To wonder if, when, how, etc.
487	**Mirar alrededor** Miró alrededor para ver si estaban allí.	To look around
488	**Más adelante** Más adelante se lo explica.	Later on, farther (or further) on
489	**Llevar la contra** Le gusta llevar la contra.	To oppose, object, raise objections, contradict.
490	**Imponerse a** Si quieres que los niños te obedezcan, tienes que imponerte a ellos.	To dominate, assert one's self over, command respect from
491	**Impedir el paso** Retírese de ahí, está usted impidiendo el paso.	To block or obstruct the way
492	**Fundarse en** ¿En qué se fundó usted para opinar de ese modo?	To base one's opinion on
493	**Figurarse que** Se figura que puede hacer todo lo que quiere.	To imagine, fancy, or guess (that)
494	**Estar hasta la coronilla de** ¡Estoy hasta la coronilla de sus bromas!	To have enough of, be fed up with
495	**En particular** Me gustan todos los deportes, pero el tenis en particular.	Particularly, especially
496	**Echar una ojeada** Le echó una ojeada al periódico.	To cast a glance, take a quick look
497	**Dar lugar a** Lo que dijo dio lugar a muchas controversias.	To cause, give rise to

498	**Costar un ojo de la cara** Nos costó un ojo de la cara.	To cost plenty
499	**Con las manos en la masa** Lo cogieron con las manos en la masa.	In the act, red-handed
500	**Al frente de** No sé quién está al frente del negocio.	In charge of, heading up
501	**A fin de que** A fin de que pudiera volver le mandó dinero.	So (that), in order that
502	**Largos años** Vivió en Nueva York largos años.	A long time, many years
503	**Tener ilusiones (de)** Tiene ilusiones de casarse algún día.	To have hopes, prospects, or illusions (of)
504	**Tener buen ojo** Ha tenido usted buen ojo al elegir ese cuadro.	To have a good eye or good foresight
505	**Puesto que** Puesto que temes aburrirte, no vayas.	Since, as long as
506	**Llegar a ser** Era muy joven cuando llegó a ser coronel.	To become, get to be
507	**Hacer referencia a** Hizo referencia a un autor muy famoso.	To refer to, make mention of
508	**Estar por** Yo estaba por ir y ellos por quedarse.	To be in favor of, be pro
509	**Estar fuera del alcance de alguien** Estaba fuera de su alcance.	To be out of or beyond someone's reach
510	**Quedarse confundido** Después de lo que dijo, me quedé confundido.	To be confused, bewildered, perplexed
511	**Enfrentarse con** No tuvo valor para enfrentarse con la situación.	To confront, stand up to, come to grips with, cope with
512	**En más de** Como se lo dije en más de una oportunidad, así pasó.	More than, for more than
513	**Dar en el clavo** Diste en el clavo con tu comentario.	To hit the nail on the head, hit the mark

514 **Disfrutar de**   To enjoy (e.g., health, comfort,
     Disfruta de todas las comodidades.   rights)

515 **Dar de baja**   To drop (from a team, list, etc.),
     Lo han dado de baja del equipo.   dismiss, discharge

516 **Cara a cara**   Right to a person's face
     Se lo dijo cara a cara.

517 **Al fin y al cabo**   After all, in the end
     Al fin y al cabo no era tan mala
     la comedia.

518 **A medio camino**   Halfway (to a place)
     Ya estamos a medio camino.

519 **A favor de**   With, aided by; (2) in favor of, in
     Remaba a favor de la corriente.   behalf of
     (2) Hizo testamento a favor de sus
     hijos.

520 **A condición de que** or **con la**   On the condition that, or the
     condición de que   understanding that, provided that
     Iré a condición de que usted vaya   (+ subjunctive)
     conmigo.

521 **Con respecto a**   With respect to, with regard to
     Quiero hablarte con respecto a mi
     nuevo empleo.

522 **Servir para**   To be used or useful for
     No sé si esto le servirá para algo.

523 **Reflexionar sobre** [or **en**]   To think over, reflect on, consider
     Reflexiona sobre lo que te dicen
     tus padres.

524 **Por lo regular**   Ordinarily, as a rule
     Por lo regular lo veía todos los días.

525 **Pasársele a uno la mano**   To go too far or to the extreme,
     A la cocinera se le pasó la mano y   overdo
     la sopa está tan salada que no se
     puede comer.

526 **Pagar en la misma moneda**   To get something back on someone,
     Me hizo pasar un mal rato; pero   give tit for tat
     le voy a pagar en la misma moneda.

527 **Hacer un paréntesis**   To digress
     Después de hacer un paréntesis,
     volvió al tema.

528 **Estar destinado a**   To be bound or destined to
     Ese proyecto está destinado a
     fracasar.

FREQ.	SPANISH	ENGLISH

529 **Estar al mando**
Está al mando del barco.

To be in command

530 **En todo caso**
En todo caso, nos vemos mañana.

Anyway, in any event

531 **En aquel entonces**
En aquel entonces mi abuelita
todavía vivía.

At that time, on that occasion

532 **Hora fija**
La función siempre empieza a
una hora fija.

Exact time, time agreed upon,
right on time

533 **Atrasado de noticias**
Me parece que usted está atrasado
de noticias.

Behind the times, ignorant of
common things

534 **Con buenos ojos**
Los nuevos estatutos no han sido
vistos con buenos ojos.

Favorably

535 **Abrirse paso** (or **camino**)
Se abría paso entre la multitud.

To make one's way

536 **Tener** (or **traer**) **retraso**
El vuelo tiene media hora de retraso.

To be late, be behind schedule

537 **Serle a uno indiferente**
Eso me es indiferente.

To make no difference to one, be
immaterial

538 **Quitarse de en medio**
Como no deseo que tengan
dificultades por mi causa, prefiero
quitarme de en medio.

To get out of the way

539 **Prestar ayuda**
¿Quiere usted prestarnos ayuda?

To help, give aid, lend a hand

540 **Pasar de largo**
Cuando vio a Juan no se paró y
pasó de largo.

To go or pass right by, pass by
without stopping

541 **Hacerse daño**
Me hice daño en el pie.

To get hurt, hurt one's self

542 **Estar a disgusto**
Estaba muy a disgusto con aquella
gente.

To be uncomfortable or ill at ease

543 **Cuando más**
Cuando más, costará treinta pesos.

At (the) most, at the outside

544 **Cosa de risa**
No es cosa de risa.

A laughing matter

545	**Corto de vista** Tiene que usar lentes porque es muy corto de vista.	Nearsighted
546	**A empujones** Había tanta gente en el circo, que tuvimos que salir a empujones.	By pushing, roughing, elbowing
547	**Tanto mejor** or **tanto peor** Tanto peor para él.	So much the better; so much the worse
548	**Sacar en limpio** No he podido sacar nada en limpio de ese discurso.	To make heads or tails of, understand, deduce
549	**Recaer sobre** La culpa siempre recae sobre el más débil.	To fall or devolve upon, revert to
550	**Por consiguiente** Por consiguiente, tenemos que aceptar su ofrecimiento.	Therefore, consequently
551	**Ni para remedio** No pude encontrar un taxi ni para remedio.	No matter how hard ones tries, not for love or money
552	**Llovido del cielo** Apareció como llovido del cielo.	Out of the clear blue sky
553	**Llevar a cabo** Llevó a cabo su misión diplomática con éxito.	To carry out, accomplish
554	**Incomodarse por** Se incomoda por cualquier cosa.	To become angry, be upset
555	**Estar frito** Estaba frito con esas preguntas.	To be annoyed
556	**Estar** (or **quedar**) **en paz** Cuando le dé tres dólares estaremos en paz.	To be even, be square
557	**Encogerse de hombros** Por toda contestación se encogió de hombros.	To shrug one's shoulders
558	**En números redondos** Los daños y perjuicios ascienden a cincuenta mil pesos, en números redondos.	In round numbers, roughly
559	**De confianza** Fue una reunión de confianza.	Informal, intimate

560   **Con detalle**   In detail
Explíquenme ustedes con detalle
como ha ocurrido eso.

561   **Caminar con pies de plomo**   To move cautiously
En este asunto hay que caminar
con pies de plomo.

562   **Así nada más**   Just plain, just as it is
—¿Adorno el pastel con figuras?
—No. Déjelo así nada más.

563   **Arreglárselas para**   To manage to
¿Cómo me las arreglaré para
terminar a tiempo?

564   **Al menos**   At least
Procure usted al menos llegar
a la hora.

565   **A la larga**   In the long run, eventually
A la larga se convencerá usted.

566   **A costa de**   At the expense of; by dint of
Lo hizo a costa de su salud.

567   **Venirse abajo** or **venirse a tierra**   To collapse, fall (through), fail
Todo aquello se vino a tierra.

568   **Saltar a la vista**   To be self-evident, obvious
Salta a la vista que los precios han
sufrido un aumento considerable.

569   **Salir del paso**   To get by, manage
Estudia sólo lo suficiente para salir
del paso.

570   **Por lo demás**   Aside from this, as to the rest
Por lo demás me parece bien.

571   **Perder el habla**   To be speechless, dumbfounded
Con la emoción perdió el habla.

572   **No tener precio**   To be much esteemed, priceless,
La ayuda que nos ha dado no tiene   valuable
precio.

573   **No tener pies ni cabeza**   To have no rhyme or reason, not
Ese proyecto no tiene pies ni cabeza. make sense, not make heads or tails

574   **Ni a tiros**   Not for anything, not for love or
No voy a hacer lo que me pidas   money
ni a tiros.

575   **Meterse a**   To take upon one's self, choose
Decidió meterse a pintor.   (e.g., a profession)

576	**Incorporarse a** Recibió órdenes de incorporarse a su batallón.	To join (e.g., a military unit, a society)
577	**Hincarse de rodillas** Lo primero que hizo fue hincarse de rodillas.	To kneel down
578	**Dar gato por liebre** Hice una mala compra. Me dieron gato por liebre.	To cheat, deceive
579	**Cuanto más** [or **menos**]... **más** [or **menos**] Cuanto más estudies, más aprenderás.	The more [or less] . . . the more [or less]
580	**Al minuto** Se hacen copias fotostáticas al minuto.	Right away, at once
581	**A prueba de** Este refugio es a prueba de bombas.	Proof against (e.g., waterproof, fireproof)
582	**A fuerza de** Lo consiguió a fuerza de trabajo.	By dint of
583	**Tomar parte** ¿Tomará parte usted en el próximo campeonato de golf?	To take part
584	**Tener en la mente** Tengo en la mente las últimas recomendaciones que me dio.	To have in mind
585	**Proceder en contra** Hay que proceder en contra de la persona culpable del incendio.	To take action against, sue
586	**Pretender decir** ¿Qué pretende usted decir?	To mean, drive at, imply
587	**Ponerse disgustado** Se pondrán muy disgustados si lo saben.	To get angry (about)
588	**Pares o** (or **y**) **nones** ¿Toma usted pares o nones?	Odds and/or evens
589	**Estar con** (or **de**) **prisa** No puedo esperar porque estoy con prisa.	To be in a hurry
590	**Enfrente de** El auto está detenido enfrente de aquel edificio.	In front of, opposite, across the way from
591	**En total** En total, lo que pasó fue esto.	In short, to sum up

592 **En principio**   In principle, fundamentally
     En principio no me parece mal la
     idea.

593 **En concreto**   Briefly, exactly, in so many words
     ¡Dime en concreto lo que haces!

594 **Decir** (or **hablar**) **entre dientes**   To mumble, mutter
     Nunca entiendo lo que me dice,
     porque siempre habla entre dientes.

595 **De un modo u otro**   In one way or another, somehow
     De un modo u otro, tenemos que
     llegar allí a la hora.

596 **Cruzarse de brazos**   To remain indifferent, be on the
     ¡Proceda a tomar una decisión   fence
     rápida; no se cruce de brazos!

597 **Como quiera que sea**   In any case, however it be
     Como quiera que sea, iremos.

598 **Al por menor**   Retail; (2) in great detail
     Vendía sólo al por menor. (2)
     Refirió al por menor todo lo
     sucedido.

599 **A lo grande**   In (great) style
     Le gustaba vivir a lo grande.

600 **Tener los huesos molidos**   To be overly tired, exhausted
     Ayer arreglé mi jardín, y hoy
     tengo los huesos molidos.

601 **Ser preciso**   To be necessary, imperative
     Es preciso llegar temprano.

602 **Ser correcto**   To be well-mannered
     Aunque no lo parece, es un joven
     muy correcto.

603 **Seguir el rastro**   To track down, trace
     La policía va a seguir el rastro del
     ladrón.

604 **Sacar partido de**   To profit or gain by
     Ese hombre saca partido de todo.

605 **Sacar a relucir**   To bring up, reveal
     Siempre saca a relucir cosas que
     sería mejor olvidar.

606 **Saber llevar el compás**   To be able to beat or keep time
     No sabe llevar el compás del mambo.   (music)

607 **Plantear una dificultad**   To pose a problem, present a
     Eso plantea una dificultad.   difficulty

608   **Obsequiar con**   To present, make a gift of
La obsequiaron con un ramo de flores.

609   **Hacerse un lío**   To get in a jam, be confused, be
He recibido tantas opiniones sobre   mixed up in
el mismo asunto, que ya me hice
un lío.

610   **Hacer furor**   To go over big, make a hit
Está haciendo furor esta nueva
canción.

611   **Estar en lo cierto**   To be right, correct
José no está seguro de estar en lo
cierto.

612   **Estar en buena disposición** (or **de**   To be in a good frame of mind
buen humor)   or mood
No le hables en este momento,
porque no está en buena disposición.

613   **Dar cuenta de**   To account for, give account of;
Hay que dar cuenta del dinero.   (2) to exhaust, finish up
(2) Dio cuenta de todo el maíz.

614   **Ante todo**   Above all
Ante todo no se olvide de escribirme.

615   **A medida que**   As, at the same time as
A medida que lleguen, dígales
usted que pasen.

616   **A ciegas**   In the dark, blindly
Se metió en ese negocio a ciegas.

617   **Sacar ventaja de**   To profit by, gain from
Sacó ventaja de ese negocio.

618   **Pues bien**   All right then
¡Pues bien, iré!

619   **Por cuenta y riesgo**   At one's own risk
Lo hizo por su cuenta y riesgo.

620   **Poner mucho ojo**   To pay (close) attention
¡Ponga usted mucho ojo en esto!

621   **Media naranja**   Better half, spouse
Ella es su media naranja.

622   **Pasarse sin**   To do or get along without
Podemos pasarnos sin motores.

623   **Idas y venidas**   Comings and goings
A pesar de tantas idas y venidas
todavía no hemos podido arreglar
ese asunto.

624   **Guiarse por**   To follow, be guided by
Quiso guiarse por los consejos de
su amigo.

625   **En caja**   On hand (said of money)
Hay que ver lo que tenemos en caja.

626   **Empeñarse en** (+ infinitive)   To persist in or be bent on
Se empeña en hacerlo a pesar de   (+ gerund), be determined to
los obstáculos.   (+ infinitive)

627   **Darse maña**   To contrive, manage
Se da maña para conseguir lo que
quiere.

628   **Conducirse como**   To act like, behave as if
Se conduce como una persona
educada.

629   **Como llovido del cielo**   Like manna from heaven
Llegó el dinero como llovido del
cielo.

630   **Ahora bien**   Now then, well now
Ahora bien, hay que aclarar este
problema.

631   **Tomarse el trabajo de**   To take the trouble to, be good
Si quieres usar mi máquina de   enough to
escribir, tómate el trabajo de venir
por ella.

632   **Todo lo posible**   Everything possible, one's utmost
Hace todo lo posible por terminar
el trabajo.

633   **Sin medida**   Without moderation, to excess
Bebe sin medida.

634   **Ser de fiar**   To be trustworthy
Ese hombre no es de fiar.

635   **Resistirse a**   To refuse to, be unwilling to
Se resistió a comer.

636   **Por entre**   Through, among, between
La vi por entre los árboles.

637   **Poner en limpio**   To make a final or clean copy
Ponga usted la carta en limpio.

638   **Pasar de (la) raya**   To go too far, exceed bounds
Procura no pasar de la raya cuando
hables en público.

639   **Mudar** (or **cambiar**) **de opinión**   To change one's mind
Mudaba de opinión todos los días.

640 **Habituarse a**
Ya me estoy habituando a comer
a las 3 de la tarde.

To accustom one's self to

641 **Estar siempre con la misma
cantaleta**
No le hagas caso, siempre está
con la misma cantaleta.

To harp on the same string, have
a one-track mind

642 **De día en día**
De día en día la situación va
empeorando.

From day to day, as time goes by

643 **Dar salida a**
Hay que dar salida a estos artículos.

To clear out, dispose of

644 **Conforme a**
Conforme a su petición...

In accordance with

645 **Con relación a**
No sé nada con relación a ese asunto.

About, concerning, with reference
or regard to, in relation to

646 **A través de**
Fueron a través del bosque.

Through, across

647 **Por intermedio de**
Lo consiguió por intermedio de su
tío.

With the help of, through, by
means of

648 **No darse por entendido**
No me di por entendido.

To pretend not to understand

649 **Ni en sueños**
No se parece a María, ni en sueños.

By no means, unthinkable

650 **Mejor que**
Mejor que escribir, ponga usted
un telegrama.

Rather than, instead of

651 **Llover a cántaros** (or **chorros**)
Espere un momento, llueve a
cántaros.

To pour, rain bucketfuls

652 **Estar** (or **hallarse**) **en el pellejo
de otro**
Después de lo que pasó, no quisiera
hallarme en el pellejo de José.

To be in somebody else's shoes

653 **Echar indirectas**
Díganos claramente qué desea que
hagamos, y deje de echar indirectas.

To make insinuations

654 **De lleno**
Su libro trataba el asunto de lleno.
(2) El golpe le dio de lleno en la cara.

Fully, adequately; (2) squarely,
right (in, on)

655 **Dar razón**   To give information
Como no estuve presente, no te
puedo dar ninguna razón.

656 **Dar a conocer**   To make known
Dio a conocer su opinión.

657 **Cara o cruz**   Heads or tails
¿A cuál le vas, cara o cruz?

658 **A falta de**   For lack of
Tomaremos esto a falta de cosa
mejor.

659 **Uno que otro**   Occasional(ly), some, a few
Uno que otro día viene a vernos.

660 **Tener a raya**   To keep within bounds, control,
La policía tenía a raya a los   restrain
ladrones.

661 **Sin fin** (**de**)   Endless, no end (of), numberless
Tenía un sin fin de cosas que hacer.

662 **Según el criterio de uno**   According to one's judgment or
Según el criterio del profesor la   way of thinking
obra tiene gran mérito.

663 **Por lo que respecta** (or **toca**) **a**   As far as . . . is concerned
Por lo que respecta a las horas de
trabajo, estoy de acuerdo con usted.

664 **Paso a paso**   Step by step, little by little
Paso a paso se hizo una posición.

665 **Haber moros en la costa**   The coast is not clear, something
Cuidado, que hay moros en la costa. is wrong

666 **Llevarse un chasco**   To be disappointed
Con esa muchacha nos llevamos un
chasco terrible.

667 **Gastar bromas pesadas**   To play practical jokes
Siempre está gastando bromas
pesadas.

668 **Fuera de quicio**   Out of one's wits
Me pone fuera de quicio con sus
necedades.

669 **Estar en plan de**   To be out for, be in the mood for
Están en plan de divertirse.

670 **Dejarse de rodeos**   To stop making excuses or
Déjese de rodeos y conteste   temporizing, stop beating around
claramente.   the bush

671	**De hecho**	In fact, as a matter of fact
	De hecho, quedó convencido.	
672	**De hoy a mañana**	Before tomorrow, any time now;
	Iré a visitarte de hoy a mañana.	when you least expect it
673	**De golpe**	Suddenly, all of a sudden
	Me lo dijo de golpe.	
674	**Dar por cierto** (or **seguro**)	To feel sure, be certain
	Doy por seguro que vendrá.	
675	**Dar fin a**	To complete, finish
	Dimos fin a la obra.	
676	**Con objeto de**	With the object or purpose of
	Fueron a París con objeto de visitar a su tía.	
677	**La niña de sus** (or **mis, tus,** etc.) **ojos**	Apple of one's eye, darling, treasure
	La quiere como a la niña de sus ojos.	
678	**A juzgar por**	Judging from or by
	A juzgar por lo que dice el periódico, el accidente fue de grandes proporciones.	
679	**Saber al dedillo**	To know perfectly or by heart
	María sabe las reglas de gramática al dedillo.	
680	**Reducirse a**	To come to, amount to, find one's self forced to
	Todo se reduce a una mala interpretación.	
681	**Estar sentido**	To be offended, hurt or peeved
	Está sentida por lo que le dijeron.	
682	**Más valiera**	Better off
	Más me valiera no haberlo conocido.	
683	**Hacer gestos**	To make faces or gestures (at), gesticulate
	Hizo gestos de aprobación.	
684	**Haber de**	To be expected or obliged to
	Hemos de llegar a tiempo.	
685	**Cuatro letras**	A few lines
	Le escribí cuatro letras.	
686	**Dejarse de historias**	To cut out the nonsense, come to the point
	Déjate de historias, y dime por qué no viniste ayer.	

687 **Dar señales de**   To show signs of
     Aunque no lo dice, da señales
     de fatiga.

688 **Dar rienda suelta a**   To give free rein to
     Dio rienda suelta a sus lágrimas.

689 **Dar la cara**   To face up (to), take
     Tuvo que dar la cara.   consequences (of)

690 **Cortar de raíz**   To nip in the bud
     Es una mala influencia y hay que
     cortarla de raíz.

691 **Contra viento y marea**   Come what may, come hell or
     Terminó sus estudios contra viento   high water
     y marea.

692 **A toda costa**   At all hazards, whatever the cost
     Lo hará a toda costa.

693 **A razón de**   At the rate of
     Pagará a razón de un seis por ciento
     al año.

694 **Recapacitar sobre**   To run over in one's mind, rethink
     Recapacitando sobre lo que me
     dijiste he decidido colaborar con
     ustedes.

695 **Levantar cabeza**   To get on one's feet
     Después de la bancarrota no pudo
     levantar cabeza.

696 **Inquietarse con, de** or **por**   To get upset about, worry about,
     Como está muy nerviosa se inquieta   be bothered by
     con cualquier ruido.

697 **Influir sobre** (or **en**)   To influence, have an influence on
     Roberto, por favor influye sobre
     María para que nos dé su aprobación.

698 **Hacer memoria**   To make an effort to recall or
     Haga usted memoria y recuerde   remember
     lo que pasó.

699 **Hacer hincapié**   To insist upon, take a firm stand
     Hizo hincapié en que debemos   against, emphasize
     llegar a la hora.

700 **Por fortuna**   Fortunately
     Por fortuna pudieron escapar.

701 **Dar una carrera**   To sprint
     Dio una carrera para alcanzarlos.

702 **Apretar el paso**   To hurry, hasten
     Apretemos el paso para llegar a
     tiempo.

703 **Velar por**   To take care of, protect
     Vela muy bien por su familia.

704 **Tomar el gusto**   To take a liking to, grow fond of
     Ya le estoy tomando el gusto a este
     juego.

705 **Salir al encuentro de**   To go out to meet
     Salió al encuentro de los invitados.

706 **Sacar jugo de**   To get a lot out of
     Saca jugo de todo lo que hace.

707 **Qué más da**   What's the difference, so what
     Si Juan no viene a la fiesta,
     ¡qué más da!

708 **Muchos recuerdos a**   Kindest regards to
     Muchos recuerdos a su familia.

709 **Lidiar con**   To contend with, have to deal with
     Si quieres, quédate a lidiar con los   (annoying, vexing persons)
     niños; yo me voy.

710 **De buenas a primeras**   Suddenly, without warning
     De buenas a primeras, empezó a
     llorar.

711 **Darle a uno coraje**   To make one angry, provoke one
     Lo que le dijeron le dio mucho
     coraje.

712 **Cosa de**   About, more or less
     Sería cosa de veinte personas.

713 **Consultar con la almohada**   To sleep on, think over
     Lo voy a consultar con la almohada.

714 **Concretarse al tema**   To confine one's self to the subject
     Por favor concrétese al tema porque
     su conferencia sólo debe durar
     media hora.

715 **Andar de prisa**   To be in a hurry, be in haste; to be
     Siempre anda de prisa.   very busy

716 **Al parecer**   Apparently
     Al parecer, vendrá la semana
     próxima.

717 **A mi ver**   In my opinion
     A mi ver, ellos tienen razón.

718   **Sin perjuicio de**   Without affecting adversely
      Procura bajar de peso; pero sin
      perjuicio de tu salud.

719   **Reflejarse en**   To reflect on, bring credit or
      Tu conducta se refleja en tu   discredit upon
      familia.

720   **Obrar en poder de**   To be in the possession of, be in the
      El expediente obra en poder   hands of
      del ministro.

721   **Rebozar de** (or **en**)   To brim over with, abound with
      Desde que la operaron del apéndice,
      está rebozando de salud.

722   **Entrar bien**   To fit, be suitable for
      Estos zapatos no me entran bien.

723   **En grande**   On a large scale
      Las fábricas están produciendo en
      grande.

724   **Dejarse llevar de la corriente**   To follow the current, go along
      En todo se deja llevar de la   with the crowd
      corriente.

725   **Dar muestras de**   To show signs or indications of
      Da muestras de entender lo que
      queremos.

726   **A menos que**   Unless
      Lo espero mañana a menos que
      usted me avise que no puede venir.

727   **Tomarle la palabra a una persona**   To take a person at his word
      Si sigue hablando seguramente le
      van a tomar la palabra.

728   **Tener disposición**   To have aptitude or talent
      Tiene mucha disposición para
      el dibujo.

729   **Hacer alarde**   To boast, brag
      Hizo alarde de valor.

730   **Ingeniárselas para**   To manage (skillfully) to
      Tengo que ingeniármelas para que
      la muchacha diga que sí.

731   **Forjarse ilusiones**   To delude one's self, build castles
      Mientras no cuentes con dinero   in the air
      suficiente para la compra del auto
      no te forjes ilusiones.

732   **Escoger al azar**   To pick out or choose at random
Escogió un número al azar.

733   **Echar un sueño**   To take a nap
A la mitad de la tarde eché un
sueño.

734   **Correr el rumor** [or **la voz**]   To be rumored, noised around
Corre el rumor de que se va a
casar.

735   **Caer en la cuenta** (**de**)   To grasp, realize, see the point of;
No caí en la cuenta hasta mucho   to think on, take note of
después.

736   **Trabar amistad**   To strike up a friendship
Trabaron amistad en un viaje.

737   **Día hábil**   Workday
¿Cuántos días hábiles hay este mes?

738   **Ponerse en camino**   To start out, to set out
Se pusieron en camino al día
siguiente.

739   **Nacer parado**   To be born lucky
Ese hombre nació parado.

740   **Llevar su merecido**   To get what's coming, get one's due
Ya era tiempo de que llevara su
merecido.

741   **Hacer presente**   To notify of, remind of
Hágale presente mi más profundo
agradecimiento.

742   **Estar desengañado**   To be disappointed or disillusioned
Están muy desengañados después
de lo ocurrido.

743   **En unas cuantas palabras**   Briefly, in a few words
Dígame lo que desea en unas
cuantas palabras.

744   **Disponerse a** [or **para**]   To get ready to, prepare one's self
Me dispongo a salir mañana.   to

745   **De categoría**   Of importance
Es un hombre de categoría.

746   **Al extremo de**   To the point of
Continuó agravándose, al extremo
de que temimos por su vida.

747   **A tal punto**   That far
A tal punto no quiero llegar.

748   **A principios de**   The first part of (a time period,
      Reunámonos a principios de la   e.g., month, year)
      semana entrante.

749   **A lo largo de**   Along, bordering, lengthwise of
      Hay un bosque a lo largo del río.

750   **Tener entre ceja y ceja**   To dislike, have a grudge against
      Mi jefe me tiene entre ceja y ceja.

751   **Nadar en la abundancia**   To live in luxury
      Desde joven nadó en la abundancia.

752   **Hacer(se) (de) la vista gorda**   To pretend not to see, wink at
      Los niños estaban robando la fruta
      pero el guardia hacía la vista
      gorda.

753   **Meter** [or **hacer**] **ruido**   To make a noise, start a row, create
      No meta usted tanto ruido.   a stir or sensation

754   **Hacer méritos**   To make one's self deserving, build
      Como empieza a trabajar, está   up good will
      haciendo méritos.

755   **En pro de**   For, in behalf of, in favor of
      Estamos en pro de que se revisen
      los estatutos.

756   **En breve plazo**   Within a short time
      Vamos a vender la casa en breve plazo.

757   **Don de gentes**   Winning manners, way of getting
      Ha tenido mucho éxito en su   on with people
      trabajo, debido en gran parte a su
      don de gentes.

758   **Dar por hecho**   To assume, take for granted
      Lo dimos por hecho.

759   **Comerse un renglón**   To skip a line
      Se ha comido un renglón.

760   **A petición de**   On or at the request of
      Esta mesa se compró a petición del
      señor Molina.

761   **Reparar en**   To consider; (2) to notice, observe
      No reparó en las consecuencias.
      (2) No reparó en el saludo que le
      hice.

762   **Obstinarse en**   To insist on, persist in
      Se obstina en quedarse en casa.

763   **No le hace**   It makes no difference, never mind,
      Eso no le hace.   it doesn't matter

764   **Guardar reserva**   To use discretion, be discreet
      Por favor, guarde usted reserva en
      esto.

765   **Errar el tiro**   To miss the mark
      Ha errado usted el tiro.

766   **En firme**   Definite, firm, binding
      Hicieron una oferta en firme.

767   **Costar un triunfo**   To be exceedingly difficult
      Nos costó un triunfo conseguirlo.

768   **Contrastar bien**   To harmonize, go well together
      Esos colores contrastan muy bien.

769   **Como quién no dice nada**   As if it were of no importance
      Habló de ganar miles de pesos
      como quién no dice nada.

770   **A toda prisa**   At full speed, with great haste
      Iban a toda prisa.

771   **A continuación**   As follows, below, continued,
      Todo se encuentra a continuación.   immediately afterwards

772   **A cada instante**   All the time, at every moment
      A cada instante esperan que estalle
      una insurrección.

773   **Sacar a luz**   To mention or bring out; to print,
      Es tiempo de sacar a luz la obra.   publish

774   **Por lo cual**   For which reason, and so, which is
      Me dijo que estabas enfermo, por   why
      lo cual te he llamado.

775   **Parar la oreja**   To prick up one's ears
      Paró la oreja para oír lo que decíamos.

776   **No despegar los labios**   To keep silent, keep one's mouth
      Estaba tan asustada que ni siquiera   shut
      podía despegar los labios.

777   **Levantar la mesa** [or **los manteles**]   To clear the table
      Levanta la mesa para que podamos
      empezar a jugar canasta.

778   **Excederse a sí mismo**   To outdo or excel one's self; to
      Quería excederse a sí mismo.   overstep, go too far

779   **Estar embriagado por**   To be overcome (with), over-
      Estaba embriagado por la emoción.   whelmed (by)

780   **Escapársele a uno**   To let something slip, say or do a
      Se me escapó la lengua. (2) Se le   thing inadvertently; (2) to miss, not
      escapó el tren.   notice, escape one's attention

781   **Echar mano de**   To resort to
       No hay más remedio que echar
       mano de todo lo que hemos ahorrado.

782   **Cortar el hilo**   To interrupt, break the thread
       Por favor, no me cortes el hilo del   (of a story)
       cuento.

783   **Con** (or **bajo**) **la mayor reserva** In strictest confidence
       Lo que acabo de decirles deben
       guardarlo bajo la mayor reserva.

784   **¿A cuánto(s) estamos?**   What is the date today?
       ¿A cuántos estamos? Estamos a
       5 de junio.

785   **Tener eco**   To spread, catch on, become
       Las palabras del señor presidente   popular
       tuvieron eco en el corazón del pueblo.

786   **Estar para**   To be about to
       Estoy para salir.

787   **Echar la llave**   To lock the door
       Eche usted la llave al salir.

788   **Cantar claro** or **cantárselas claras** To speak with outright frankness,
       Tendré que cantárselo claro.   tell straight from the shoulder

789   **Andar a caza de**   To go hunting for, go in search of
       Los periodistas andaban a caza de
       noticias.

790   **A lo más**   At (the) most
       A lo más, costará diez pesos.

791   **A la vuelta de**   Upon returning from
       A la vuelta de mi viaje nos veremos.

792   **Ni soñar**   Not by any means, not by a long
       ¿Te lo doy? ¡Ni soñar!   shot, far from it

793   **Echar una mano**   To lend a hand, help out
       ¿Por qué no nos echas una mano?

794   **A quemarropa**   Point-blank, at very close range
       Le disparó dos tiros a quemarropa.

795   **A pedir de boca**   According to desire
       Todo salió a pedir de boca.

796   **A decir verdad**   Frankly, to tell the truth
       A decir verdad, yo no creo eso.

797   **Tener pesar**   To be sorry for or about
       Tengo gran pesar por lo que hice.

798   **Tener detenido (algo)**   To be holding (something) up
      Por falta de papel membretado
      tiene detenido el trabajo.

799   **Ser (algo) un decir**   To be just a myth, saying, manner
      La eterna primavera en México   of speaking
      es sólo un decir.

800   **Pretender demasiado (de)**   To make unreasonable demands
      Esa señora pretende demasiado de   (on), ask too much (of)
      su cocinera.

801   **Levantar planos**   To draw up plans
      Los ingenieros levantaron un plano
      para un nuevo muelle.

802   **Entrar en materia**   To come to the point, get down to
      Deje de discutir y entremos en   business.
      materia.

803   **Desprenderse de**   To give away
      Se ha desprendido de toda su
      fortuna.

804   **Dar guerra**   To make trouble, cause annoyance
      Dile a los chicos que no den guerra.

805   **Siempre armar líos**   To always make trouble, confusion,
      Siempre arma líos.   or difficulties; raise a rumpus
                                                    habitually

806   **Tomar cuerpo**   To take shape
      El proyecto va tomando cuerpo.

807   **Tener la pena de**   To have the misfortune to
      Tuvo la pena de perder a su
      padre.

808   **No caber en sí de gozo**   To be beside one's self with joy, be
      Desde que ganó el concurso, está   overcome
      que no cabe en sí de gozo.

809   **Inclinarse a**   To be inclined to, be favorably
      Me parece que se inclina a hacerlo.   disposed toward

810   **Dar marcha atrás**   To go into reverse, back up
      No dé marcha atrás, que hay un
      árbol.

811   **Con buenos modos** or **con malos**   Politely, with good manners; rudely,
      modos   with bad manners
      Contestó con muy malos modos.

812   **A grandes rasgos** (or **pinceladas**)   Briefly, in outline, in a few words
      Se lo contaré a grandes rasgos.

813   **Tener (mucho) mundo**   To be sophisticated or experienced
      José tiene mucho mundo.

814   **Decir bien**   To be right, correct
      Dice usted bien.

815   **Fuera de sí**   Beside one's self
      Estaba fuera de sí de cólera.

816   **De una vez y para siempre**   Once and for all
      De una vez y para siempre, se lo
      prohibo.

817   **Poner reparo(s)**   To make or raise objection(s)
      ¿Puso algún reparo a aquella carta?

818   **Mirar por**   To look after, take care of
      ¿No tienen a nadie que mire por
      ellos?

819   **Matar de aburrimiento**   To be bored to death, bored stiff
      Ese trabajo me mata de
      aburrimiento.

820   **Guardarse de**   To avoid, guard against, keep from
      Guárdese de las malas compañías.

821   **El reverso de la medalla**   Just the opposite, the opposite in
      Juan es muy formal, pero su   every respect
      hermano es precisamente el reverso
      de la medalla.

822   **De trecho en trecho**   At intervals
      Han plantado árboles de trecho en
      trecho.

823   **Apresurar la marcha**   To hurry, speed up
      Hay que apresurar la marcha.

824   **De dirección única** or **de un solo   One-way
      sentido**
      Esta calle es de dirección única.

825   **Variar de** (or **en**) **opinión**   To change one's mind
      Es de mujeres variar de opinión.

826   **Tomar mala voluntad**   To have a grudge against
      A partir de ese momento le tomó
      mala voluntad.

827   **Morderse la lengua**   To hold or control one's tongue
      Al no tener que responder, se
      mordió la lengua.

828   **Estar próximo a**   To be just about to, be almost to
      Estuvo próximo a caerse al río.

829	**Estar a merced de** Estamos a merced de la tempestad.	To be at the mercy of, be at the expense of
830	**Deshacerse en lágrimas** No le hables así porque se va a deshacer en lágrimas.	To melt or break into tears
831	**Dar forma a** Había que darle forma al artículo.	To put in final form or shape
832	**A** (or **según**) **mi entender** A mi entender, la situación no es tan desfavorable como parece.	In my opinion, according to my understanding
833	**Por encima** Leí el documento por encima.	Superficially, hastily
834	**Poner pleito** Como resultado del accidente, José va a poner pleito a Juan por manejar en forma descuidada.	To sue, bring suit or charges against
835	**Poner de relieve** Puso de relieve las cualidades de su invitado de honor.	To point out, emphasize, make stand out
836	**Lleno de bote en bote** La sala estaba llena de bote en bote.	Clear full, full to the brim
837	**A rienda suelta** Se rio a rienda suelta.	Without restraint
838	**Poco más o menos** Saldremos poco más o menos a las ocho de la mañana.	More or less, about
839	**Saber a gloria** Comimos un pastel que sabía a gloria.	To be delicious
840	**Írsele a uno la lengua** Se le va la lengua muy fácilmente.	To let something out (by talking), be loose-tongued, give one's self away
841	**En todos los tonos** Se lo he dicho en todos los tonos.	In every possible way
842	**Ser de rigor** Es de rigor visitar este lugar.	To be indispensable, required by custom
843	**Latirle a uno** Me late que se va a enojar.	To have a premonition or hunch
844	**Cuesta abajo** or **cuesta arriba** Para mí sería cuesta arriba tratar de aprender chino.	Downhill, (to be) easy; uphill, (to be) difficult

845   **Ser blando de corazón**   To be softhearted
No va a castigarlo duramente;
es muy blando de corazón.

846   **Según y conforme** (or **como**)   It depends, according as
Se lo diré según y conforme tú me
lo dices.

847   **Mirar con fijeza**   To stare at
Se quedó mirando al niño con fijeza.

848   **Decir por decir**   To talk for the sake of talking
No hace más que decir por decir.

849   **Dar la lata**   To annoy, bother, pester
Nos daba la lata con sus quejas.

850   **No omitir esfuerzos**   To spare no efforts
No omitió esfuerzo alguno para
ayudarlos.

851   **Inducir a error**   To lead into error
Estas instrucciones no son claras,
y pueden inducir a error.

852   **En eso estriba la dificultad**   There's where the trouble lies
No tenemos ganas de hacerlo, y en
eso estriba la dificultad.

853   **Atender razones**   To listen to reason
Siempre hace lo que quiere; nunca
atiende razones.

854   **Armar una bronca**   To pick a quarrel, start a fight
Como Juan había bebido demasiado,
armó una bronca.

855   **Hoy por hoy**   For the time being, at present
Hoy por hoy el trabajo sigue sin
hacer.

856   **Dar la nota discordante**   To be the disturbing or trouble-
Dio la nota discordante con su   some element
comentario.

857   **Pagar los vidrios rotos**   To be punished undeservingly, be
No es justo que usted tenga que   made the scapegoat
pagar los vidrios rotos.

858   **No morderse la lengua**   Not to mince words, speak straight
No se muerde la lengua para decir   from the shoulder
lo que piensa.

859   **Tener trazas**   To show signs, give indications
Esto no tiene trazas de terminar.

860 **Meter en cintura**   To discipline, restrain, hold back
Hay que meter en cintura a ese
chico.

861 **Devanarse los sesos**   To rack one's brains
Me estoy devanando los sesos para
encontrar una solución.

862 **Andar** (or **ir**) **de capa caída**   To be disheartened, be on the
¡Pobrecillos, andan de capa caída!   downgrade, be in a bad way (in
                                              business, health, etc.)

863 **A más no poder**   To the utmost, as hard as possible
Estudia a más no poder.

864 **De peso**   Weighty, of importance
El señor es una persona de peso.

865 **A todo**   All out, to the limit
Iban a todo correr.

866 **Tomarla con**   To pick at or on, to fight with, to
Ya veo que estás furiosa pero no   have a grudge against
la tomes conmigo.

867 **Presencia de ánimo**   Presence of mind, calm, cool
Su presencia de ánimo nos salvó
del peligro.

868 **Identificarse con**   To identify one's self with, become
Este novelista se identifica con sus   involved with
personajes.

869 **Estar** [or **quedar**] **en los huesos**   To be nothing but skin and bones
Si sigue poniéndose a dieta pronto
va a estar en los huesos.

870 **Tener la mira puesta en**   To aim at, have as a goal
Tiene la mira puesta en ese trabajo.

871 **No darle a uno frío ni calor**   To leave one indifferent
No me daba frío ni calor.

872 **En un descuido**   When least expected
En un descuido llega.

873 **Al romper el día** (or **el alba**)   At dawn, at daybreak
Los pájaros empiezan a cantar
cuando rompe el día.

874 **Al habla** (**con**)   [To get] in touch (with)
Te recomiendo que te pongas al
habla con María a la brevedad posible.

875 **Ser menester**   To be necessary
No es menester que venga a verme.

876 **Dar oídos**   To listen, lend an ear
     No quiso dar oídos a aquello.

877 **A todo trance**   At any cost, cost what it may
     Está resuelto a hacerlo a todo trance.

878 **Abstraer(se) en**   To concentrate, be lost in thought
     Está abstraída en sus propios
     pensamientos.

879 **En suma**   In short, in brief
     En suma, ¿qué es lo que pasó?

880 **Así como así**   Anyway, anyhow, just like that, as
     No se lo digo así como así.   simply as all that, without reason

881 **A la corta o a la larga**   Sooner or later
     Los veremos a la corta o a la larga.

882 **Prevalecer sobre**   To prevail against or over, outshine,
     Su actidud anterior prevalece sobre   surpass
     la que está tomando ahora.

883 **Contrastar mal**   To clash (e.g., colors)
     Esos colores contrastan mal.

884 **Aflojar las riendas a**   To give rein to, relax watchfulness
     No sea tan riguroso con sus   or authority over
     empleados; aflójeles las riendas.

885 **Sin ningún género de duda**   Without any doubt, beyond a
     Carmen va a ganar el premio sin   shadow of a doubt
     ningún género de duda.

886 **Romper a**   To begin, burst out, suddenly
     Rompió a hablar cuando nadie lo   start to
     esperaba.

887 **Llenar** (or **colmar**) **la medida**   To be the last straw
     Eso colma la medida.

888 **Escurrirse de entre las manos**   To slip out of or through one's
     ¡Qué lástima! El florero de cristal   hands (or fingers)
     se me escurrió de las manos.

889 **Extremarse en** (+ infinitive)   To strive hard to
     Los del partido de la oposición se
     han extremado en manifestar sus
     ideas.

890 **A** (or **por**) **la inversa**   On the contrary, contrariwise, the other
     Sucedió a la inversa, Juan se fue a   way around
     Europa y José se quedó.

891 **En hora buena**   Safely, luckily; all right, OK
     En hora buena decidí tomar este
     curso.

| 892 | **Tomar el rábano por las hojas** | To put the cart before the horse |

892 **Tomar el rábano por las hojas**   To put the cart before the horse
Desgraciadamente, a menudo toma
el rábano por las hojas.

893 **Tener mercado con**   To trade with
Tenemos mercado con toda América.

894 **Ser una perla**   To be a jewel or treasure
Esa criada es una perla.

895 **Para el interior de uno**   To one's self
Lo dijo para su interior.

896 **Mirar de lado**   To look askance at, look down
Aquella mujer me miró de lado.   upon

897 **Entrar a empellones**   To push one's way in
La gente entraba a empellones.

898 **De mal grado**   Unwillingly, reluctantly
Aceptó de mal grado.

899 **A título de información**   Unofficially, off the record
Los datos que le di son solamente
a título de información.

900 **Ser de provecho**   To be good (for)
Esta comida es de mucho provecho
para usted.

901 **No estar de gracia** (or **para gracias**)   To be in no mood for joking
No me molestes, que no estoy para
gracias.

902 **A modo de**   A sort of, a kind of
Pusimos un pedazo de madera en la
puerta, a modo de cerradura.

903 **Sin reposo**   Ceaselessly, endlessly
Habla sin reposo.

904 **Ser de la mayor conveniencia**   To be highly desirable
Sería de la mayor conveniencia
que viniera usted.

905 **Ponerse a la obra**   To get to work
Pongámonos a la obra.

906 **Levantarse del lado izquierdo**   To be irritable, get up on the
Todo me ha salido mal hoy. No   wrong side of the bed
cabe duda que me levanté del lado
izquierdo.

907 **Entre bastidores**   Behind the scenes
Deben estar tramando algo entre
bastidores.

908   **Estar en buen uso**   To be in good condition
      Ese abrigo está todavía en buen uso.

909   **Echarse sobre las espaldas**   To take on, to assume as a
      Creo que no debes echarte sobre   responsibility
      las espaldas el cuidado de tres
      sobrinos.

910   **Conocerle a uno el juego**   To be onto someone
      No va creer lo que le digas, porque
      ya te conoce el juego.

911   **Bien inclinado** or **mal inclinado**   Well-disposed, good-natured;
      Todo niño es bien o mal inclinado   ill-disposed, bad-natured
      según la educación que ha
      recibido.

912   **Andarse por las ramas**   To beat around the bush
      No te andes por las ramas y dime
      si vas a ir o no.

913   **Dar por descontado**   To take for granted
      Puedes dar por descontado que
      vendrá.

914   **Por igual**   Evenly, uniformly, equally
      Compartieron todo por igual.

915   **Hacerle salir los colores a uno**   To make one blush
      Le hizo salir los colores a la cara
      con lo que dijo.

916   **Estar reconocido por las atenciones**   To be grateful for one's kindness
      Estoy reconocido por sus
      atenciones.

917   **Trabajar como una fiera**   To work like a dog
      Siempre trabaja como una fiera.

918   **Doblar la hoja**   To change the subject
      Este asunto es bastante delicado,
      doblemos la hoja.

919   **Es fama que**   It is said, known, or rumored that
      Es fama que en España hay muchos
      gitanos.

920   **A saber**   Namely, that is, specifically
      Son tres: a saber, Enrique, Juan y
      María.

921   **A centenares**   By the hundreds
      Murieron las gentes a centenares.

922	**Escurrir el bulto**	To sneak away, slip away
	Escurrió el bulto cuando menos lo pensábamos.	
923	**Echar(lo) todo a rodar**	To upset everything carelessly, spoil things
	Tiene tan poco tino que por lo general lo echa todo a rodar.	
924	**Resarcirse de**	To make up for
	Si se saca la lotería va a resarcirse de toda su pérdida.	
925	**Tocante a**	About, concerning, with reference or regard to, touching on
	Háblame por teléfono mañana tocante al alquiler de la casa.	
926	**Mejor que mejor**	All the better, so much the better
	Si viene, mejor que mejor.	
927	**Al primer golpe de vista**	At first glance, at first sight
	Al primer golpe de vista me pareció más grande.	
928	**No dejar piedra por** (or **sin**) **mover**	To leave no stone unturned
	Investiguen cuidadosamente. No dejen piedra sin mover.	
929	**Echar de ver**	To notice, observe
	No echó de ver el cambio.	
930	**Con arreglo a**	According to, in accordance with
	Lo hicimos con arreglo a sus instrucciones.	
931	**Caer en la red**	To fall into the trap
	Están tratando de que cometas un error. Procura no caer en la red.	
932	**A todas luces**	Any way you look at it, by all means
	A todas luces es cierto.	
933	**Rezar con**	To concern or affect, have to do with
	La orden no reza conmigo.	
934	**Mucho ruido y pocas nueces**	Much ado about nothing
	Todo parece indicar que la obra va a ser un éxito. Sin embargo creo que hay mucho ruido y pocas nueces.	
935	**Diciendo y haciendo**	And so doing
	Diciendo y haciendo se puso a cantar.	
936	**Doblar la cabeza**	To give in, yield
	Dobló la cabeza y aceptó ser el único culpable de todo lo que había sucedido.	

937 **A ese** (or **tal**) **efecto**
A ese efecto voy a escribirle una
carta.

For that (or such) purpose, to
that (or such) end

938 **Tener precisión**
Tengo precisión de salir.

To need (to), have (to)

939 **Sin ponderación**
Sin ponderación, él es el mejor
guitarrista que he conocido.

Without the slightest exaggeration

940 **Sin faltar una jota**
Se aprendió el discurso sin faltar
una jota.

In minutest detail

941 **Preciarse de**
Se precia de su habilidad.

To take pride in, boast of

942 **Leer entre renglones**
Leí entre renglones que prefería no
asistir a la boda.

To read between the lines

943 **De intento**
Sabes que el niño está enfermo,
y de intento haces todo el ruido
que puedes.

On purpose

944 **Pintarse solo para**
Se pinta solo para ser jefe.

To have great talent, flair, or
aptitude for

945 **Todo bicho viviente**
Se lo contó a todo bicho viviente.

Every living soul, everyone under
the sun

946 **Salvarse en una tabla**
Estuvo a borde de la muerte; pero
se salvó en una tabla.

To have a narrow escape

947 **Punto de gracia**
Tiene su punto de gracia.

Funny side

948 **A la postre**
A la postre tuvieron que renunciar
al viaje.

At last, in the long run

949 **Traer de cabeza a uno**
Los últimos acontecimientos me
traen de cabeza.

To drive one crazy

950 **Cosido a las faldas de**
Esa niña siempre está cosida a las
faldas de su mamá.

Tied to the apron strings of

951 **Sin qué ni para qué**
Hizo un largo viaje sin qué ni para
qué.

Without any reason, cause, or
motive

952	**Sobre la marcha** Hay que hacer las enmiendas sobre la marcha.	Simultaneously, at the same time
953	**Como el más pintado** Puede hacerlo como el más pintado.	As (with) the best of them
954	**A la luz de** A la luz de los últimos acon- tecimientos podemos ver cuál es la verdadera situación.	In (the) light of
955	**Estar agotado** Después de esa caminata estoy agotado.	To be exhausted, be completely tired out
956	**Echar los bofes** Estoy echando los bofes de cansado.	To throw one's self into a job, work hard; to be out of breath
957	**Para su gobierno** Le hago esta advertencia para su gobierno.	For your guidance
958	**Aguzar los oídos** [or **el oído**] Se paró detrás de la puerta y aguzó el oído.	To prick up one's ears, listen intently
959	**Tocar en lo vivo** Mis palabras lo tocaron en lo vivo.	To hurt (one) deeply, cut to the quick
960	**Renunciar a sí mismo** Renunció a sí mismo y ya no insistió más.	To deny one's self
961	**Tener sus más y sus menos** Como todas las cosas, vivir en el centro tiene sus más y sus menos.	To have one's good and bad points
962	**Cortar** (or **recortar**) **al prójimo** Le gusta mucho recortar al prójimo.	To criticize, find fault
963	**Dar largas** Siempre le está dando largas al asunto del viaje a Europa.	To procrastinate, delay, put off; to give (one) the runaround
964	**Calentarse los cascos** Aunque se caliente usted los cascos no lo resolverá.	To rack one's brains
965	**Al presente** Al presente no tenemos ninguna noticia.	At present, right now
966	**Afilar** (or **aguzar**) **el ingenio** Si aguzas el ingenio puedes encontrar la solución adecuada.	To sharpen one's wits

967   **Estar de vena**   To be in the mood
       No estoy de vena para hacer versos
       ahora.

968   **Quedársele a uno algo en el tintero**   To forget a thing completely or
       Se me ha quedado en el tintero.   entirely

969   **Hacer ascos de**   To turn up one's nose at, pretend
       Le hace ascos a todo.   to be contemptuous of

970   **El mejor día**   Some fine day (ironic)
       El mejor día se presenta aquí.

971   **Ser mano**   To be first, lead out
       Cuando empecemos a jugar, yo
       quiero ser mano.

972   **De fijo**   Surely, without doubt
       De fijo llueve hoy.

973   **Mal que le** (or **me, te,** etc.) **pese**   Whether he (or I, you, etc.) likes it
       Tenemos que declinar el honor,   or not, however much it may
       mal que nos pese.   displease him (or me, you, etc.)

974   **Muy noche**   Late at night
       Era muy noche cuando regresamos.

975   **De punta en blanco**   All dressed up, in full regalia
       Iban de punta en blanco.

976   **Por fórmula**   As a matter of form
       Le saludó por fórmula.

977   **A punto fijo**   Exactly, with certainty, for sure
       No lo sé a punto fijo.

978   **Según mi leal saber y entender**   To the best of my knowledge
       Eso no está bien hecho según mi
       leal saber y entender.

979   **Hacer puente**   To take the intervening day off
       El próximo viernes no se trabaja;
       por lo tanto podemos hacer puente.

980   **Poner en observancia**   To enforce in a most conscientious
       El último reglamento de tránsito   fashion
       ha sido puesto en observancia.

981   **En mengua de**   To the discredit of
       Todos esos falsos rumores van a
       resultar en mengua de su reputación.

982   **Correr** [or **echar**] **un velo** (**sobre**)   To drop (the matter), hush
       Corramos un velo sobre el asunto   (something) up
       del robo.

983   Ni por el forro   Not [to know] in the slightest
Parece que María no conoce los
buenos modales ni por el forro.

984   Estar en lo firme   To be in the right
Creo que estoy en lo firme.

985   A toda vela   Under full sail, at full speed
El noviazgo marcha a toda vela.

986   Ni con mucho   Not by any means, not by a long
No es, ni con mucho, tan trabajadora   shot, far from it
como su hermana.

987   A poca costa   With little effort
Lo consiguió a poca costa.

988   Decir a todo amén   To be a yes-man
Dice a todo amén.

989   Mirar de hito en hito   To eye up and down, stare at
Se quedó mirándolo de hito en hito.

990   A reserva de   With the intention of
Te envío esta tarjeta a reserva de
escribirte después una carta muy
larga.

991   Tener en poco   To hold in low esteem, be
El tiene en poco los méritos de su   scornful of
contrincante.

992   A lo vivo   With vivid description
Se lo pintó a lo vivo.

993   Decir para sí   To reason, say to one's self
Se dijo para sí que no le convenía
aceptar.

994   Por sus puños   By one's self, on one's own
El sitio que tiene lo ha ganado
por sus puños.

995   Estar a la mira   To be on the lookout
Procura estar a la mira por si
vienen.

996   Tener a gala   To be proud of, glory in, take
Tenía a gala ser guatemalteco.   pride in

997   A ratos perdidos   In spare time, in leisure hours
Este vestido lo hice a ratos perdidos.

998   Hacerle un feo a uno   To be impolite to one, slight one
Vaya usted a visitarlo, no le haga
usted un feo.

999   **Hacerle a uno un flaco servicio**   To play a dirty trick on one
      Le hizo un flaco servicio.

1000 **Caerse por** [or **de**] **su** (**propio**) **peso**   To be self-evident, be obvious, go
      Eso se cae por su propio peso.   without saying

PART 2
SPANISH ALPHABETICAL LISTING

In the alphabetical arrangement of the 1,000 idioms, all punctuation, including parentheses, is ignored. The listing is word by word, short before long, as in most library card catalogs. For example, all idioms beginning with the single one-letter word *a* are listed at the beginning, and the longer word *abierto* is filed after *a última hora*. Similarly, *encargarse de* appears after *en voz baja,* and *estar entendido que* after *estar en vísperas de.*

Where the English translation of the idiom is an infinitive, "to" is omitted.

Alternate forms of an idiom are listed separately, each in its appropriate alphabetical order. For instance, *aún no* appears under the *a*'s, and its variant, *todavía no,* under the *t*'s. Where such separate alphabetical listing results in adjacent entries for the variant forms, however — as in the case of *correr el rumor* [or *la voz*], for example — they are left together as one entry. Exceptions are the idioms whose alternate versions result in entirely different meanings. For example, *en voz alta* (out loud) and *en voz baja* (in a soft voice), although they are variants of the same idiom, are given separate adjacent listings.

After each idiom is its frequency-of-occurrence number, by which a Spanish vernacular example, a more complete English translation, where advisable, and other pertinent information can be found in part one.

SPANISH	FREQ.	ENGLISH
A cada instante	772	All the time, at every moment
A cambio de	238	In exchange or trade for
A carta cabal	15	Thoroughly, in every respect
A centenares	921	By the hundreds
A ciegas	616	In the dark, blindly
A conciencia	399	Conscientiously, painstakingly
A condición de que	520	On the condition or understanding that
A continuación	771	As follows, continued
A costa de	566	At the expense of; by dint of
¿A cuánto(s) estamos?	784	What is the date today?
A decir verdad	796	Frankly, to tell the truth
A duras penas	160	With great difficulty
A empujones	546	By pushing, elbowing

SPANISH	FREQ.	ENGLISH
A escondidas de	425	Without the knowledge of
A ese efecto	937	For that purpose, to that end
A falta de	658	For lack of
A favor de	519	With, aided by; in favor of, in behalf of
A fin de que	501	So (that), in order that
A fines de	236	Toward the end of (week, month, etc.)
A fondo	475	Thoroughly, fully
A fuerza de	582	By dint of
A grandes rasgos (or **pinceladas**)	812	Briefly, in outline, in a few words
A juzgar por	678	Judging from or by
A la carrera	423	On the run, hastily, hurriedly
A la corta o a la larga	881	Sooner or later
A la fuerza	424	By force, forcibly
A la inversa	890	On the contrary, the other way around
A la larga	565	In the long run, eventually
A la luz de	954	In (the) light of
A la moda	398	Fashionable, in style
A la postre	948	At last, in the long run
A la vez	327	At once, simultaneously
A la vuelta de	791	Upon returning from
A lo grande	599	In (great) style
A lo largo de	749	Along, bordering, lengthwise of
A lo lejos	296	In the distance, way over there
A lo más	790	At (the) most
A lo mejor	187	As luck may have it, like as not
A lo vivo	992	With vivid description
A mano	186	By hand; within reach; (be) even
A más no poder	863	To the utmost, as hard as possible

SPANISH	FREQ.	ENGLISH
A más tardar	138	At the latest
A mediados de	235	Around the middle of (week, month, etc.)
A medida que	615	As, at the same time as
A medio camino	518	Halfway (to a place)
A medio hacer	185	Half done, incomplete
A menos que	726	Unless
A menudo	326	Often, frequently
A mi entender	832	In my opinion, according to my understanding
A mi (or **tu, su,** etc.) **modo**	458	In my (or your, etc.) own way
A mi ver	717	In my opinion
A modo de	902	A kind of
A pedir de boca	795	According to desire
A pesar de	271	In spite of, despite
A petición de	760	At the request of
A poca costa	987	With little effort
A principios de	748	The first part of (a time period, e.g., month, year)
A propósito	91	By the way; on purpose
A prueba de	581	Proof against (e.g., fireproof, waterproof)
A punto fijo	977	Exactly, for sure
A que...	319	I'll bet . . .
A quemarropa	794	Point blank, at very close range
A ratos perdidos	997	In spare time, in leisure hours
A razón de	693	At the rate of
A reserva de	990	With the intention of
A rienda suelta	837	Without restraint
A saber	920	Namely, that is, specifically
A tal efecto	937	For such purpose, to such end
A tal punto	747	That far
A título de información	899	Unofficially, off the record
A toda costa	692	At all hazards, whatever the cost

SPANISH	FREQ.	ENGLISH
A toda prisa	770	At full speed, with great haste
A toda vela	985	Under full sail, at full speed
A todas luces	932	Any way you look at it, by all means
A todo	865	All out, to the limit
A todo trance	877	At any cost, cost what it may
A través de	646	Through, across
A última hora	159	At the last moment, in the nick of time
Abierto de par en par	237	Wide open
Abrirle los ojos a uno	477	Open someone's eyes; disabuse someone
Abrirse paso (or **camino**)	535	Make one's way
Abstraer(se) en	878	Concentrate, be lost in thought
Acabar de	39	Have just
Acerca de	310	About, having to do with
Acusar recibo de	457	Acknowledge receipt of
Además de	295	In addition to
Advertir algo a alguien	264	Tell one (so)
Afilar el ingenio	966	Sharpen one's wits
Aflojar las riendas a	884	Give rein to, relax watchfulness or authority over
Aguzar el ingenio	966	Sharpen one's wits intently
Aguzar los oídos [or **el oído**]	958	Prick up one's ears, listen
Ahora bien	630	Now then, well now
Ahora mismo	210	At once, right away; just, just now
Al contrario	158	On the other hand, on the contrary
Al derecho	397	Right side out
Al extremo de	746	To the point of
Al fin	157	At last, finally
Al fin y al cabo	517	After all, in the end
Al frente de	500	In charge of, heading up
Al habla (**con**)	874	[Get] in touch (with)

SPANISH	FREQ.	ENGLISH
Al menos	564	At least
Al minuto	580	Right away, at once
Al parecer	716	Apparently
Al pie de la letra	351	Word for word, thoroughly
Al por mayor	156	Wholesale, in large quantity
Al por menor	598	Retail; in great detail
Al presente	965	At present, right now
Al primer golpe de vista	927	At first glance, at first sight
Al principio	114	At first, at the outset
Al revés	55	The opposite; wrong side (inside) out
Al romper el día (or **el alba**)	873	At dawn, at daybreak
Alegrarse de	38	Be glad or happy about (something)
Algo por el estilo	294	Something like that, something of the kind
Alguna vez	234	Sometimes, now and then, every so often
Andar a caza de	789	Go hunting for, go in search of
Andar de capa caída	862	Be on the downgrade, be in a bad way
Andar de prisa	715	Be in a hurry; be very busy
Andarse por las ramas	912	Beat around the bush
Ante todo	614	Above all
Apresurar la marcha	823	Hurry, speed up
Apretar el paso	702	Hurry, hasten
Aprovechar la ocasión	325	Take advantage of the situation
Aquí mismo	370	Right here
Armar una bronca	854	Pick a quarrel, start a fight
Arreglárselas para	563	Manage to
Ascender a	456	Amount to (in money); be promoted to
Así como así	880	Anyway, anyhow, as simply as all that, without reason
Así nada más	562	Just plain, just as it is

SPANISH	FREQ.	ENGLISH
Atender razones	853	Listen to reason
Atrasado de noticias	533	Behind the times, ignorant of common things
Aún no	94	Not yet

B

Bajo la mayor reserva	783	In strictest confidence
Bien inclinado	911	Well-disposed, good-natured
Boca abajo	232	Face down, on one's stomach
Boca arriba	232	Face upward, on one's back
Buen genio	239	Good nature or temper
¡Buen provecho!	270	Good appetite!
Burlarse de	293	Make fun of, poke fun at

C

Caer en la cuenta (de)	735	Realize, see the point of; think on, take note of
Caer en la red	931	Fall into the trap
Caerse por [or **de**] **su** (**propio**) **peso**	1000	Be self-evident, be obvious, go without saying
Calentarse los cascos	964	Rack one's brains
Cambiar de opinión	639	Change one's mind
Caminar con pies de plomo	561	Move cautiously
Cantar claro or **cantárselas claras**	788	Speak with outright frankness, tell straight from the shoulder
Cara a cara	516	Right to a person's face
Cara o cruz	657	Heads or tails
Cerca de	455	Near (location); nearly, about, almost
Colmar la medida	887	Be the last straw
Comerse un renglón	759	Skip a line
Como el más pintado	953	As (with) the best of them
Como llovido del cielo	629	Like manna from heaven
Como quién no dice nada	769	As if it were of no importance

Spanish	Freq.	English
Como quiera que sea	597	In any case, however it be
Como una fiera	454	Like a wild beast, furious(ly)
Compadecerse de alguien (or **algo**)	324	Pity, sympathize with, feel sorry for someone (or something)
Comunicarse con	419	Get in touch with
Con arreglo a	930	According to, in accordance with
Con buenos modos	811	Politely, with good manners
Con buenos ojos	534	Favorably
Con destino a	369	Bound for, going to
Con detalle	560	In detail
Con intención	453	Deliberately, knowingly
Con la condición de que	520	On the condition or understanding that
Con la mayor reserva	783	In strictest confidence
Con las manos en la masa	499	In the act, red-handed
Con malos modos	811	Rudely, with bad manners
Con mucho gusto	72	Gladly, willingly
Con objeto de	676	With the object or purpose of
Con permiso	292	If you don't mind, with your permission, please excuse me
Con relación a	645	About, in relation to
Con respecto a	521	With respect to, with regard to
Con tal que	208	Provided that, in the event that
Con tiempo	209	In (good) time, in advance
Concretarse al tema	714	Confine one's self to the subject
Conducirse como	628	Act like, behave as if
Confiar en	153	Rely on, trust in
Conforme a	644	In accordance with
Conocerle a uno el juego	910	Be onto someone
Consistir en	396	Be a question or matter of
Constar de	452	Be composed of, consist of
Constarle a uno	309	Be evident to one

Spanish	Freq.	English
Consultar con la almohada	713	Sleep on, think over
Contar con	184	Depend upon, count on
Contentarse con	350	Be satisfied or happy with
Contra viento y marea	691	Come what may, come hell or high water
Contrastar bien	768	Go well together, harmonize
Contrastar mal	883	Clash (e.g., colors)
Convenirle a uno	291	Be to one's advantage, be advisable
Correr el rumor [or **la voz**]	734	Be rumored, noised around
Correr peligro	349	Run a risk
Correr por cuenta de uno	290	Be one's affair, be up to one
Correr riesgo	183	Chance, run risk
Correr un velo (**sobre**)	982	Drop (the matter), hush (something) up
Cortar al prójimo	962	Criticize, find fault
Cortar de raíz	690	Nip in the bud
Cortar el hilo	782	Interrupt, break the thread (of a story)
Corto de vista	545	Nearsighted
Cosa de	712	About, more or less
Cosa de risa	544	A laughing matter
Cosa (**digna**) **de ver**	412	Something worthwhile or worth seeing
Cosido a las faldas de	950	Tied to the apron strings of
Costar mucho trabajo	150	Be difficult
Costar un ojo de la cara	498	Cost plenty
Costar un triunfo	767	Be exceedingly difficult
Cruzarse de brazos	596	Remain indifferent, be on the fence
Cuando más	543	At (the) most, at the outside
Cuando quiera	113	Whenever or as soon as you would like, when you are ready
Cuanto antes	395	As soon as possible
Cuanto más [or **menos**]... **más** [or **menos**]	579	The more [or less] . . . the more [or less]

Cuatro letras	685	A few lines
Cuesta abajo	844	Downhill, (be) easy
Cuesta arriba	844	Uphill, (be) difficult

D

Dar a conocer	656	Make known
Dar a entender	348	Pretend; insinuate, drive at
Dar a luz	368	Give birth (to)
Dar ánimo	474	Cheer up, buoy up
Dar cuenta de	613	Account for, give account of; exhaust, finish up
Dar cuerda a	93	Wind (a watch, clock, toy)
Dar de baja	515	Drop (from a team, list, etc.), dismiss, discharge
Dar disgustos a	182	Cause distress or grief to
Dar el pésame por	14	Present or give one's condolences (for, on), extend one's sympathy (for, on)
Dar en	367	Hit; take to
Dar en el clavo	513	Hit the nail on the head, hit the mark
Dar facilidades	207	Facilitate, offer every assistance
Dar fin a	675	Complete, finish
Dar forma a	831	Put in final form or shape
Dar gato por liebre	578	Cheat, deceive
Dar guerra	804	Make trouble, cause annoyance
Dar la cara	689	Face up (to), take the consequences (of)
Dar la lata	849	Annoy, bother
Dar la nota discordante	856	Be the disturbing or troublesome element
Dar la razón	269	Agree (with), acknowledge (a person) to be right
Dar la vuelta a algo	154	Turn or rotate something; go around something

Spanish	Freq.	English
Dar largas	963	Procrastinate, delay; give (one) the runaround
Dar las gracias	2	Thank, be grateful
Dar lástima	92	Arouse pity or regret
Dar lugar a	497	Cause, give rise to
Dar marcha atrás	810	Go into reverse, back up
Dar mucha pena	155	Make one sorry, be disconcerting
Dar muestras de	725	Show signs or indications of
Dar oídos	876	Listen, lend an ear
Dar parte	268	Inform, notify, report
Dar por cierto	674	Feel sure, be certain
Dar por descontado	913	Take for granted
Dar por hecho	758	Assume, take for granted
Dar por seguro	674	Feel sure, be certain
Dar que decir (or **hablar**)	366	Cause criticism
Dar que hacer	54	Make or cause (extra) work
Dar rabia	151	Anger, make furious
Dar razón	655	Give information
Dar rienda suelta a	688	Give free rein to
Dar salida a	643	Clear out, dispose of
Dar señales de	687	Show signs of
Dar un paseo	233	Take a walk or stroll
Dar una carrera	701	Sprint
Dar una mano	231	Apply (a coat of paint, varnish, etc.); help out, lend a hand
Dar una vuelta	13	Walk, take a stroll
Darle a uno coraje	711	Make one angry, provoke one
Darle a uno la gana	219	Feel like, want to
Darle a uno lo mismo	206	Be all the same to one
Darle a uno vergüenza	95	Be ashamed, be (too) bashful or shy
Darse cuenta de	152	Realize, be aware of
Darse maña	627	Contrive, manage
Darse prisa	323	Hurry, move quickly

De acuerdo con	181	In accordance or agreement with
De ahora en adelante	70	From now on, in the future
De aquí en adelante	112	From now on, henceforth
De broma	47	As a joke, in jest
De buena fe	180	In good faith, with complete confidence
De buena gana	289	Willingly, with pleasure
De buenas a primeras	710	Suddenly, without warning
De categoría	745	Of importance
De confianza	559	Informal, intimate
De cuando en cuando	473	From time to time, occasionally
De día en día	642	From day to day, as time goes by
De dirección única	824	One-way
¿De dónde?	347	How? Whence? By what means?
De enfrente	37	Across (the street), directly opposite, in front (of)
De esta manera (or **este modo**)	205	This way, in this manner
De etiqueta	230	Formal, full dress
De fijo	972	Surely, without doubt
De golpe	673	All of a sudden
De hecho	671	In fact, as a matter of fact
De hoy a mañana	672	Any time now; when you least expect it
De hoy en adelante	112	From now on, henceforth
De intento	943	On purpose
De la noche a la mañana	149	Overnight, all at once
De lado	418	Sideways, on its side
De lleno	654	Fully, adequately; squarely
De lo contrario	229	Otherwise, if not
De lo lindo	179	Very much, greatly, wonderfully
De mal en peor	88	From bad to worse
De mal grado	898	Unwillingly, reluctantly

Spanish	Freq.	English
De mala fe	180	With no confidence
De mala gana	289	Unwillingly, reluctantly
De manera que	472	So that, as a result
De más	71	Too much, too many
De memoria	5	By heart, from memory
De modo que	265	So, and so; so that
De ningún modo	322	By no (any) means, under no (any) circumstances
De ninguna manera	148	By no means, under no circumstances
De nuevo	24	Again, once more
De paso	417	In transit; in passing
De peso	864	Weighty, of importance
De pronto	321	Abruptly, all of a sudden
De punta en blanco	975	All dressed up, in full regalia
De pura casualidad	199	Purely by chance
De repente	147	All of a sudden, unexpectedly
De todas maneras	31	At any rate, in any event
De trecho en trecho	822	At intervals
De un día para otro	288	From one day to the next, day by day
De un modo u otro	595	In one way or another, somehow
De un solo sentido	824	One-way
De una vez y para siempre	816	Once and for all
Decidirse a	36	Make up one's mind to
Decir a todo amén	988	Be a yes-man
Decir bien	814	Be right, correct
Decir entre dientes	594	Mumble, mutter
Decir para sí	993	Reason, say to one's self
Decir por decir	848	Talk for the sake of talking
Dejar de	69	Stop, cease
Dejar dicho	266	Leave word
Dejar en paz	137	Leave alone, let be
Dejarle a uno plantado	416	Leave one in the lurch; stand someone up

Dejarse de cuentos	414	Come to the point, stop beating around the bush
Dejarse de historias	686	Cut out the nonsense, come to the point
Dejarse de rodeos	670	Stop making excuses or temporizing, stop beating around the bush
Dejarse llevar de la corriente	724	Follow the current, go along with the crowd
Delante de	52	In the presence of, in front of
Dentro de	53	Inside (of); in or within (a period of time)
Dentro de poco	87	Soon, shortly
Desde abajo	415	From below
Desde ahora	287	From now on, beginning now
Desde entonces	146	Since then
Desde fuera	471	From the outside
Desde hace	23	For, over a period of, dating from
Desde lejos	204	From a distance, from afar
Desde luego	413	Of course, naturally
Desde que	136	Ever since, from the moment that
Desde un principio	226	Right from the start or beginning
Deshacerse en lágrimas	830	Melt or break into tears
Desprenderse de	803	Give away
Después de	135	After, following
Detrás de	86	Behind
Devanarse los sesos	861	Rack one's brains
Día hábil	737	Workday
Dicho y hecho	476	No sooner said than done
Diciendo y haciendo	935	And so doing
Digno de confianza	178	Reliable, trustworthy
Dirigir la palabra	346	Address, speak
Disculparse por	308	Apologize for

Disfrutar de	514	Enjoy (e.g., health, comfort, rights)
Disponer de	344	Spend, squander; have at one's disposal
Disponerse a [or **para**]	744	Get ready to, prepare one's self to
Doblar la cabeza	936	Give in, yield
Doblar la hoja	918	Change the subject
Don de gentes	757	Winning manners, way of getting on with people

E

Echar a perder	51	Spoil, go to waste
Echar al correo	307	Mail, post (letters, etc.)
Echar de menos	177	Miss, long for
Echar de ver	929	Notice, observe
Echar indirectas	653	Make insinuations
Echar la culpa a	267	Lay the blame on
Echar la llave	787	Lock the door
Echar los bofes	956	Throw one's self into a job, work hard; be out of breath
Echar mano de	781	Resort to
Echar todo a rodar	923	Upset everything carelessly, spoil things
Echar un sueño	733	Take a nap
Echar un velo (**sobre**)	982	Drop (the matter), hush (something) up
Echar una mano	793	Lend a hand, help out
Echar una ojeada	496	Cast a glance, take a quick look
Echar(lo) todo a rodar	923	Upset everything carelessly, spoil things
Echarse a (**reír, llorar,** etc.)	261	Begin, burst out, suddenly start to (laugh, cry, etc.)
Echarse atrás	394	Back out, withdraw
Echarse sobre las espaldas	909	Take on, assume as a responsibility

Spanish	Freq.	English
El día menos pensado	134	When one least expects
El mejor día	970	Some fine day (ironic)
El reverso de la medalla	821	Just the opposite, the opposite in every respect
Empeñarse en	626	Be bent on, be determined to, persist in
Empleársele bien a uno	111	Serve someone right, get one's due
En aquel entonces	531	At that time, on that occasion
En breve plazo	756	Within a short time
En broma	47	As a joke, in jest
En caja	625	On hand (money)
En calidad de	450	In the capacity of, as
En cambio	110	But, on the other hand
En cierta manera (or **forma**)	449	In a way
En concreto	593	Briefly, exactly, in so many words
En cuanto	68	As soon as
En cuanto a	365	Regarding, having to do with
En efecto	345	In fact, right
En el extranjero	89	Abroad, out of the country
En el fondo	85	At heart, by nature
En eso estriba la dificultad	852	There's where the trouble lies
En favor	343	In or on behalf (of)
En fila	133	In (a) line
En fin	306	In short; well (expletive)
En firme	766	Definite, firm, binding
En grande	723	On a large scale
En hora buena	891	Safely, luckily; all right, OK
En la actualidad	227	At the present time, right now
En la mitad (**de**)	132	In the middle of
En lo alto de	339	On top of
En lo futuro	393	In or for the future, hereafter
En lo posible	448	As far or as much as possible
En lugar de	67	Instead of, in place of

Spanish	Freq.	English
En mangas de camisa	262	In shirt sleeves
En más de	512	More than, for more than
En mengua de	981	To the discredit of
En números redondos	558	In round numbers, roughly
En observación	447	Under observation
En particular	495	Particularly, especially
En presencia de	263	In front of, before
En primer lugar	203	In the first place
En principio	592	In principle, fundamentally
En pro de	755	For, in behalf of, in favor of
En punto	22	On the dot, exactly
En regla	411	In order
En representación de	145	As an emissary of, representing
En resumidas cuentas	144	In short, in a word
En suma	879	In short, in brief
En tal caso	341	In such a case or instance
En todo caso	530	Anyway, in any event
En todos los tonos	841	In every possible way
En total	591	In short, to sum up
En un abrir y cerrar de ojos	392	In a very short time, in the twinkling of an eye
En un descuido	872	When least expected
En un dos por tres	260	In a jiffy, quickly
En unas cuantas palabras	743	Briefly, in a few words
En vano	84	In vain
En vez de	108	Instead of, rather than
En voz alta	176	Out loud
En voz baja	176	In a soft voice
Encargarse de	83	Take charge of, assume responsibility for
Encogerse de hombros	557	Shrug one's shoulders
Enfrentarse con	511	Confront, come to grips with
Enfrente de	590	In front of, opposite, across the way from
Enorgullecerse de	446	Pride one's self on, boast of

Spanish	Freq.	English
Enterarse de	259	Find out or learn about, become aware of
Entrar a empellones	897	Push one's way in
Entrar bien	722	Fit, be suitable for
Entrar en materia	802	Come to the point, get down to business
Entre bastidores	907	Behind the scenes
Entusiasmarse con	175	Be enthusiastic about
Equivocarse de	35	Be mistaken or wrong about (something)
Errar el tiro	765	Miss the mark
Es decir	174	That is to say, in other words
Es fama que	919	It is said, known, or rumored that
Escapársele a uno	780	Say or do a thing inadvertently; not notice, escape one's attention
Escoger al azar	732	Pick out or choose at random
Escurrir el bulto	922	Sneak away, slip away
Escurrirse de entre las manos	888	Slip out of or through one's hands (or fingers)
Esforzarse en, por, or **para**	364	Strive to
Está bien or **está bueno**	1	All right, correct, OK
Estar a cargo	202	Be in charge
Estar a disgusto	542	Be uncomfortable or ill at ease
Estar a gusto	297	Be comfortable, contented, as one likes it
Estar a la expectativa de	470	Be on the lookout for
Estar a la mira	995	Be on the lookout
Estar a merced de	829	Be at the mercy of, be at the expense of
Estar a punto de	286	Be at the point of, be about to
Estar al mando	529	Be in command
Estar agotado	955	Be exhausted
Estar con	82	Have (an illness or discomfort)
Estar con ánimo de	340	Have a mind or notion to
Estar con prisa	589	Be in a hurry

Estar de acuerdo	66	Agree
Estar de buen humor	612	Be in a good frame of mind or mood
Estar de luto	12	Be in mourning, bereavement
Estar de malas	305	Be out of luck
Estar de moda	21	Be popular, fashionable, stylish
Estar de prisa	589	Be in a hurry
Estar de sobra	320	Be in the way, be superfluous
Estar de turno	258	Be on duty
Estar de vena	967	Be in the mood
Estar de viaje	285	Be traveling, be on the road
Estar desengañado	742	Be disappointed or dis-illusioned
Estar destinado a	528	Be bound or destined to
Estar embriagado por	779	Be overcome with, over-whelmed by
Estar en buen uso	908	Be in good condition
Estar en buena disposición	612	Be in a good frame of mind or mood
Estar en deuda con	342	Be indebted or obliged to
Estar en el pellejo de otro	652	Be in somebody else's shoes
Estar en las nubes	201	Daydream, muse
Estar en lo cierto	611	Be right, correct
Estar en lo firme	984	Be in the right
Estar en los huesos	869	Be nothing but skin and bones
Estar en paz	556	Be even, be square
Estar en plan de	669	Be in the mood for
Estar en un error	338	Be mistaken, wrong
Estar en vigor	445	Be in effect, in force
Estar en vísperas de	444	Be on the eve of, be about to
Estar entendido que	131	Be understood or agreed (that)
Estar frito	555	Be annoyed
Estar fuera del alcance de alguien	509	Be out of or beyond someone's reach

SPANISH	FREQ.	ENGLISH
Estar hasta la coronilla de	494	Have enough of, be fed up with
Estar muy metido en	200	Be deeply involved in
Estar para	786	Be about to
Estar por	508	Be in favor of, be pro
Estar prevenido	257	Be prepared, forewarned
Estar próximo a	828	Be just about to
Estar reconocido por las atenciones	916	Be grateful for one's kindness
Estar rendido	130	Be exhausted
Estar sentido	681	Be offended, hurt or peeved
Estar siempre con la misma cantaleta	641	Harp on the same string, have a one-track mind
Estarse muriendo por	363	Be dying to, be anxious to
Estrechar la mano (a)	410	Shake hands (with)
Excederse a sí mismo	778	Outdo or excel one's self; overstep, go too far
Extrañarle a uno	198	Seem strange to one
Extremarse en	889	Strive hard to

Faltar a	49	Absent one's self from, miss; show disrespect to
Fiar(se) en, a or **de**	337	Rely on, trust in
Figurarse que	493	Imagine, fancy, or guess (that)
Fijarse en	81	Pay attention to, mark one's word
Forjarse ilusiones	731	Delude one's self, build castles in the air
Formar parte de	255	Be a member or part of
Frente a	34	In front of
Frente a frente	109	Face to face
Fuera de quicio	668	Out of one's wits
Fuera de sí	815	Beside one's self
Fundarse en	492	Base one's opinion on

Spanish	Freq.	English
Ganar tiempo	362	Save time
Ganarse la vida	4	Earn or make a living
Gastar bromas pesadas	667	Play practical jokes
Gracias a	188	Thanks to
Guardar reserva	764	Use discretion, be discreet
Guardarse de	820	Avoid, guard against
Guiarse por	624	Follow, be guided by

Spanish	Freq.	English
Haber de	684	Be expected or obliged to
Haber moros en la costa	665	The coast is not clear, something is wrong
Habituarse a	640	Accustom one's self to
Hablar entre dientes	594	Mumble, mutter
Hablar hasta por los codos	284	Chatter, talk idly
Hacer alarde	729	Boast, brag
Hacer algo a medias	469	Do something poorly, do a halfway job
Hacer ascos de	969	Turn up one's nose at
Hacer buen papel	225	Make a good showing
Hacer buenas migas	50	Get along well together, be congenial
Hacer caso a	48	Pay attention to, obey
Hacer caso de	173	Pay attention to, respect
Hacer cola	29	Stand in line, line up
Hacer de cuenta (que)	443	Pretend (that), act as if
Hacer (de) la vista gorda	752	Pretend not to see, wink at
Hacer escala	391	Land, make a stop
Hacer falta	80	Be necessary; have need of, lack
Hacer frente a	390	Face up to, confront
Hacer furor	610	Make a hit, go over big

SPANISH	FREQ.	ENGLISH
Hacer gestos	683	Make faces or gestures (at)
Hacer gracia	304	Strike one (as) funny
Hacer hincapié	699	Insist upon, take a firm stand against
Hacer juego	283	Match, go well (with)
Hacer mal papel	225	Make a poor showing
Hacer memoria	698	Make an effort to recall or remember
Hacer méritos	754	Make one's self deserving, build up goodwill
Hacer presente	741	Notify of, remind of
Hacer puente	979	Take the intervening day off
Hacer referencia a	507	Refer to, make mention of
Hacer ruido	753	Make a noise, start a row, create a stir
Hacer un mandado	282	Run an errand
Hacer un paréntesis	527	Digress
Hacerle a uno un flaco servicio	999	Play a dirty trick on one
Hacerle daño a uno	107	Hurt or be harmful to one; not agree (physically) with one
Hacerle salir los colores a uno	915	Make one blush
Hacerle un feo a uno	998	Be impolite to one, slight one
Hacerse daño	541	Get hurt, hurt one's self
Hacer(se) (de) la vista gorda	752	Pretend not to see, wink at
Hacerse de noche	389	Get dark
Hacerse el sordo	256	Refuse to consider, turn a deaf ear
Hacerse el tonto	197	Play dumb, act the fool
Hacerse ilusiones	254	Deceive or fool one's self
Hacerse rogar	280	Be coaxed, importuned
Hacerse tarde	33	Become late, be getting late
Hacerse un lío	609	Get in a jam, be confused, be mixed up in
Hallarse en el pellejo de otro	652	Be in somebody else's shoes
Hasta aquí	228	So far, up to now
Hasta cierto punto	129	To a certain point or extent

Spanish	Freq.	English
Hasta la fecha	32	Up to now, to date
Hay gato encerrado	420	There is more than meets the eye
Hay que	9	It is necessary to (that)
Hecho a la medida	422	Made to order or measure, custom-made
Hecho y derecho	143	Mature, grown-up, full-fledged
Hincarse de rodillas	577	Kneel down
Hora fija	532	Time agreed upon, right on time
Hoy en día, or **hoy día**	388	These days, nowadays
Hoy por hoy	855	For the time being, at present

Spanish	Freq.	English
Ida y vuelta	28	Round-trip, two-way
Idas y venidas	623	Comings and goings
Identificarse con	868	Identify one's self with, become involved with
Ilusionarse con	387	Get excited about, get up one's hopes about
Impedir el paso	491	Block or obstruct the way
Imponerse a	490	Dominate, command respect from
Importarle a uno	79	Matter or be of importance to one, concern one
Inclinarse a	809	Be inclined to, be favorably disposed toward
Incomodarse por	554	Become angry, be upset
Incorporarse a	576	Join (e.g., a military unit, a society)
Inducir a error	851	Lead into error
Influir sobre (or **en**)	697	Influence (verb)
Informarse de	318	Find out about, gather information on
Ingeniárselas para	730	Manage (skillfully) to

SPANISH	FREQ.	ENGLISH
Inquietarse con, de or por	696	Get upset about, worry about
Ir a medias	196	Go fifty-fifty, go halves
Ir al grano	409	Get to the point
Ir de capa caída	862	Be on the downgrade, be in a bad way
Ir de compras	11	Go shopping, do marketing
Ir del brazo	78	Walk arm in arm
Irle a uno bien [or mal]	361	Be becoming [or unbecoming]
Írsele a uno la lengua	840	Be loose-tongued, give one's self away

J

Jugarse el todo por el todo	442	Bet everything
Juntarse con	451	Associate with

L

La mayor parte (de)	46	The majority (of)
La niña de sus (or mis, tus, etc.) ojos	677	Apple of one's eye, darling
Lado flaco	386	Weak side or spot
Largos años	502	A long time, many years
Latirle a uno	843	Have a premonition or hunch
Leer entre renglones	942	Read between the lines
Lejos de	224	Far from, far removed from, distant from
Levantar cabeza	695	Get on one's feet
Levantar la mesa [or los manteles]	777	Clear the table
Levantar planos	801	Draw up plans
Levantarse del lado izquierdo	906	Be irritable, get up on the wrong side of the bed
Librarse de	303	Get rid of, escape from, avoid
Lidiar con	709	Contend with
Limitar con	142	Be bounded or bordered by; be held down or back
Lo de menos	45	Of little importance, insignificant

Spanish	Freq.	English
Lo indicado	360	That which is stated or requested
Llamar la atención	105	Attract attention, call attention to; reprimand, censure, chide
Llegar a ser	506	Become, get to be
Llegar a suceder	468	Come to pass, happen
Llenar la medida	887	Be the last straw
Lleno de bote en bote	836	Clear full, full to the brim
Llevar a cabo	553	Carry out, accomplish
Llevar la contra	489	Oppose, raise objections, contradict
Llevar la delantera	467	Be ahead, have the lead
Llevar puesto	223	Be wearing (clothes or jewelry)
Llevar su merecido	740	Get what's coming, get one's due
Llevar ventaja	385	Be ahead, have a lead
Llevarse bien con	128	Get along well with
Llevarse un chasco	666	Be disappointed
Llover a cántaros (or **chorros**)	651	Pour, rain bucketfuls
Llovido del cielo	552	Out of the clear blue sky

M

Spanish	Freq.	English
Mal genio	239	Bad disposition or temper
Mal inclinado	911	Ill-disposed, bad-natured
Mal que le (or **me, te,** etc.) **pese**	973	Whether he (or I, you, etc.) likes it or not
¡Manos a la obra!	359	Let's get to work!
Más adelante	488	Later on, farther (or further) on
Más allá (**de**)	253	Farther on, beyond
Más bien	408	Rather, preferably
Más valiera	682	Better off
Matar de aburrimiento	819	Be bored to death, bored stiff
Matar dos pájaros de [or **en**] **un tiro**	407	Kill two birds with one stone
Matar el tiempo	405	Kill or waste time
Media naranja	621	better half, spouse

Spanish	Freq.	English
Mejor dicho	104	Or rather, better yet
Mejor que	650	Rather than, instead of
Mejor que mejor	926	All the better, so much the better
Menos de	127	Fewer than, less than
Merecer la pena	252	Be worthwhile
Meter en cintura	860	Discipline, restrain, hold back
Meter ruido	753	Make noise, start a row, create a stir
Meterse a	575	Take upon one's self, choose (e.g., a profession)
Meterse con	281	Pick a fight with
Meterse en lo que no le importa	65	Be (too) inquisitive, butt in
Mientras más... más	251	The more . . . the more
Mientras menos... menos	251	The less . . . the less
Mientras no	250	Unless, if not
Mientras tanto	64	Meanwhile
Mirar alrededor	487	Look around
Mirar con fijeza	847	Stare at
Mirar de hito en hito	989	Eye up and down, stare at
Mirar de lado	896	Look askance at, look down upon
Mirar por	818	Look after, take care of
Molestarse en	317	Bother about, take the trouble to
Morderse la lengua	827	Hold or control one's tongue
Mucho ruido y pocas nueces	934	Much ado about nothing
Muchos recuerdos a	708	Kindest regards to
Mudar de opinión	639	Change one's mind
Muy noche	974	Late at night

N

Spanish	Freq.	English
Nacer parado	739	Be born lucky
Nada de particular	222	Nothing special, nothing unusual

Spanish	Freq.	English
Nadar en la abundancia	751	Live in luxury
Negarse a	221	Refuse to, decline to
Negocio redondo	384	Good or sound bargain
Ni a tiros	574	Not for anything, not for love or money
Ni con mucho	986	Not by a long shot
Ni en sueños	649	By no means, unthinkable
Ni mucho menos	466	Far from it, or anything like it
Ni para remedio	551	No matter how hard one tries, not for love or money
Ni por el forro	983	Not [know] in the slightest
Ni siquiera	249	Not even, not a single
Ni soñar	792	Not by a long shot
Ninguna parte	194	Nowhere, not any place
No cabe duda (de que)	406	There's no doubt or uncertainty (that)
No caber en sí de gozo	808	Be beside one's self with joy, be overcome
No dar el brazo a torcer	248	Be stubborn, unyielding
No darle a uno frío ni calor	871	Leave one indifferent
No darse por entendido	648	Pretend not to understand
No dejar piedra por (or **sin**) **mover**	928	Leave no stone unturned
No despegar los labios	776	Keep silent, keep one's mouth shut
No estar de gracia (or **para gracias**)	901	Be in no mood for joking
No hay de qué	44	Don't mention it, you're welcome
No hay más remedio que	220	There's nothing to do but
¡No hay pero que valga!	441	No buts about it!
No hay que darle vueltas	440	There are no two ways about it
No le hace	763	It makes no difference, never mind
No morderse la lengua	858	Not mince words, speak straight from the shoulder
No omitir esfuerzos	850	Spare no efforts

SPANISH	FREQ.	ENGLISH
No poder con	336	Not be able to stand, endure, control
No poder ver a alguien	103	Not be able to tolerate someone
No poder ver ni en pintura	76	Not be able to stand the sight of
No saber dónde meterse	404	Not know which way to turn
No sea que	335	Or else, lest
No ser cosa de juego	316	Not be a laughing matter
No ser ni la sombra de uno	140	Be but a shadow of one's former self
No tener pelos en la lengua	314	Be outspoken, unreserved in speech
No tener pies ni cabeza	573	Not make sense, not make heads or tails
No tener precio	572	Be much esteemed, priceless, valuable
No tener remedio	315	Be beyond repair, help, or recourse

O

Obrar en poder de	720	Be in the possession of, be in the hands of
Obsequiar con	608	Present, make a gift of
Observar buena conducta	439	Behave well
Obstinarse en	762	Insist on, persist in
Ocuparse de	102	Take care of, attend to
Ocurrírsele a uno	30	Occur to one, cross one's mind
Oír hablar de	62	Hear about
Oponer resistencia	438	Offer resistance
Otra vez	10	Again, once more, another time

P

Pagar a plazos	61	Pay in installments
Pagar en la misma moneda	526	Get something back on someone, give tit for tat

Spanish	Freq.	English
Pagar los gastos	172	Pay the expenses, foot the bill
Pagar los vidrios rotos	857	Be punished undeservingly, be made the scapegoat
Para el interior de uno	895	To one's self
Para su gobierno	957	For your guidance
Parar la oreja	775	Prick up one's ears
Parece mentira	43	It hardly seems possible, it appears to be impossible
Parecido a	60	Like, similar to
Pares o (or **y**) **nones**	588	Odds and/or evens
Participar de	437	Share (in)
Pasado de moda	171	Out of date, out of style
Pasar de la raya	638	Go too far, exceed bounds
Pasar de largo	540	Go or pass right by, pass by without stopping
Pasar de raya	638	Go too far, exceed bounds
Pasar el rato	126	Kill time, pass the time away
Pasar por alto	218	Overlook, forget, gloss or pass over
Pasar revista a	436	Review, go over carefully
Pasar un buen rato	42	Have a good time
Pasarse sin	622	Do or get along without
Pasársele a uno	383	Get over (a state of mind); forget (to)
Pasársele a uno la mano	525	Go too far or to the extreme, overdo
Paso a paso	664	Step by step, little by little
Pedir prestado	101	Borrow, ask to lend
Pensar de	125	Think of, have an opinion of or about
Pensar en	3	Think about; intend
Perder de vista	358	Lose sight of
Perder el habla	571	Be speechless, dumbfounded
Perder el hilo de	382	Lose the thread of
Perder la cabeza	279	Lose one's head (colloq.)
Perder la vista	381	Go blind, lose one's vision

Spanish	Freq.	English
Perderse de vista	124	Be lost from sight, vanish
Pesarle a uno	278	Regret, be sorry for
Pintarse solo para	944	Have great talent, flair, or aptitude for
Plan de estudios	170	Curriculum, set of courses
Plantear una dificultad	607	Pose a problem, present a difficulty
Poco a poco	20	Little by little, gradually
Poco después (de)	141	Soon after, a little after
Poco más o menos	838	More or less, about
Poner a uno al corriente (de)	357	Inform one, tell one, bring one up to date
Poner de relieve	835	Point out, emphasize
Poner el grito en el cielo	106	Make a great fuss, hit the ceiling
Poner en claro	356	Clear up, unravel
Poner en limpio	637	Make a final or clean copy
Poner en marcha	380	Start, put in motion
Poner en observancia	980	Enforce in a most conscientious fashion
Poner en ridículo	302	Make a fool of, humiliate
Poner la mesa	6	Set the table
Poner mucho ojo	620	Pay (close) attention
Poner pleito	834	Sue, bring suit or charges against
Poner reparo(s)	817	Make or raise objection(s)
Ponerse a	217	Begin to, start out to
Ponerse a la obra	905	Get to work
Ponerse colorado	301	Blush
Ponerse de acuerdo	123	Come to an agreement, be in accord
Ponerse de pie	195	Get up, stand, arise
Ponerse disgustado	587	Get angry (about)
Ponerse en camino	738	Start out, set out
Ponerse en contra de	313	Oppose, be against
Ponérsele a uno carne de gallina	379	Get gooseflesh

Spanish	Freq.	English
Por adelantado	63	Beforehand, in advance
Por ahora	59	For the present
Por aquí cerca	122	Around here, in the vicinity
Por casualidad	19	By chance, by the way, incidentally
Por consiguiente	550	Therefore, consequently
Por cuenta y riesgo	619	At one's own risk
Por dentro	168	Inside, within
Por detrás	435	From behind; behind one's back
¿Por dónde?	167	Which way? Where?
Por encima	833	Superficially, hastily
Por encima de	355	Above, over
Por entre	636	Through, among, between
Por eso	166	For that reason, therefore
Por extenso	18	In detail, at great length
Por fin	139	At last, finally
Por fórmula	976	As a matter of form
Por fortuna	700	Fortunately
Por fuera	77	On the outside
Por hoy	421	For the present
Por igual	914	Evenly, uniformly, equally
Por intermedio de	647	With the help of, through, by means of
Por la inversa	890	On the contrary, the other way around
Por la mitad	216	In half, in the middle
Por las buenas	247	Willingly, of one's own accord
Por las buenas o por las malas	334	Whether one likes it or not
Por las nubes	165	Sky-high, extreme
Por lo cual	774	For which reason, and so, which is why
Por lo demás	570	Aside from this, as to the rest
Por lo general	300	Usually, in general, ordinarily
Por lo menos	27	At least, leastwise

Por lo pronto	434	For the time being, in the meantime
Por lo que respecta (or **toca**) **a**	663	As far as . . . is concerned
Por lo regular	524	Ordinarily, as a rule
Por lo visto	41	Apparently, evidently
Por más que	246	However much, no matter how much
Por ningún lado	194	Nowhere, not any place
Por ningún motivo	164	Under no circumstances, no matter what
Por ninguna parte	194	Nowhere, not any place
Por otra parte	193	On the other hand
Por poco	58	Almost
Por primera vez	57	For the first time
Por regla general	378	As a general rule, usually
Por si acaso	163	Just in case, if by chance
Por supuesto	121	Of course, certainly
Por sus puños	994	By one's self, on one's own
Por término medio	430	On the average
Por última vez	100	Finally, for the last time
Por un lado... por otro	192	On the one side (or hand) . . . on the other, in a way . . . in another way
Preciarse de	941	Take pride in, boast of
Preguntar por	26	Inquire about, ask for (a person)
Preguntarse se, cuándo, cómo, etc.	486	Wonder if, when, how, etc.
Prender fuego a	333	Set on fire
Preocuparse por	25	Worry about, be concerned for or about
Presencia de ánimo	867	Presence of mind, calm, cool
Prestar atención	277	Pay attention, be alert
Prestar ayuda	539	Help, give aid, lend a hand
Prestarse a	433	Lend itself to; offer to
Presumir de	485	Consider one's self to be
Pretender decir	586	Mean, drive at, imply

Pretender demasiado (de)	800	Make unreasonable demands (on), ask too much (of)
Prevalecer sobre	882	Prevail against or over, outshine, surpass
Prevenirse contra	377	Take precautions against
Proceder en contra	585	Take action against, sue
Pues bien	618	All right then
Puesto que	505	Since, as long as
Punto de gracia	947	Funny side
Punto de vista	215	Point of view, standpoint
Punto por punto	484	Step by step, in detail

Q

Qué más da	707	What's the difference, so what
Quedar bien con	332	Make a hit with, get along with
Quedar en	120	Agree on, come to a mutual understanding about
Quedar en or **de**	483	Agree to, promise to
Quedar en los huesos	869	Be nothing but skin and bones
Quedar en paz	556	Be even, be square
Quedar entendido que	131	Be understood or agreed (that)
Quedar mal con	332	Not make a hit with, not get along with
Quedarse con	75	Take (as in choosing or buying); remain or stay with
Quedarse confundido	510	Be confused, bewildered
Quedársele a uno algo en el tintero	968	Forget a thing completely or entirely
Querer decir	17	Mean
Quitarse de en medio	538	Get out of the way
Quitarse un peso de encima	191	Take a load off one's mind, be relieved

Spanish	Freq.	English
Rebozar de (or **en**)	721	Brim over with, abound with
Recaer sobre	549	Fall or devolve upon, revert to
Recapacitar sobre	694	Run over in one's mind, rethink
Recomendar algo a uno	169	Make a special request of someone for something; entrust something to someone
Recortar al prójimo	962	Criticize, find fault
Reducirse a	680	Come to, amount to, find one's self forced to
Referirse a	190	Refer to, have reference to
Reflejarse en	719	Reflect on, bring credit or discredit upon
Reflexionar sobre [or **en**]	523	Think over, reflect on, consider
Refrescar la memoria	354	Refresh one's memory
Relacionarse con	402	Have dealings with
Rendir cuentas a (or **ante**)	162	Give or render an accounting to
Renunciar a sí mismo	960	Deny one's self
Reparar en	761	Consider; notice, observe
Resarcirse de	924	Make up for
Resistirse a	635	Refuse to, be unwilling to
Responder por	245	Be responsible for or vouch for (a person)
Rezar con	933	Concern or affect, have to do with
Rodearse de	432	Surround one's self with
Romper a	886	Begin, burst out, suddenly start to

S

Spanish	Freq.	English
Saber a	482	Have the flavor of, taste like
Saber a gloria	839	Be delicious

Spanish	Freq.	English
Saber al dedillo	679	Know perfectly or by heart
Saber de sobra	376	Be fully aware
Saber en qué se queda	465	Find out where one stands
Saber lo que es bueno	244	Know what one is missing, know what is going on
Saber llevar el compás	606	Be able to beat or keep time (music)
Sacar a luz	773	Mention or bring out; print, publish
Sacar a relucir	605	Bring up, reveal
Sacar en claro	431	Clear up, come to a conclusion
Sacar en limpio	548	Make heads or tails of, understand, deduce
Sacar jugo de	706	Get a lot out of
Sacar partido de	604	Profit or gain by
Sacar ventaja de	617	Profit by, gain from
Salir al encuentro de	705	Go out to meet
Salir del paso	569	Get by, manage
Salir ganando	243	Come out ahead, win
Salirse con la suya	299	Have or get one's way
Saltar a la vista	568	Be self-evident, obvious
Salvarse en una tabla	946	Have a narrow escape
Seguir el rastro	603	Track down, trace
Seguir los pasos a	480	Keep an eye on, check
Según el criterio de uno	662	According to one's judgment or way of thinking
Según mi entender	832	In my opinion, according to my understanding
Según mi leal saber y entender	978	To the best of my knowledge
Según parece	464	As it seems, apparently
Según y conforme (or **como**)	846	It depends, according as
Sentir en el alma	189	Regret deeply, be terribly sorry
Sentirse molesto	429	Be annoyed, bothered
Ser aficionado a	242	Be a fan or avid follower of
Ser (algo) un decir	799	Be just a myth, saying, manner of speaking

Spanish	Freq.	English
Ser bien recibido	463	Be well taken or received
Ser blando de corazón	845	Be softhearted
Ser correcto	602	Be well-mannered
Ser de fiar	634	Be trustworthy
Ser de la mayor conveniencia	904	Be highly desirable
Ser de lamentar	401	Be regrettable, distressing, too bad
Ser de provecho	900	Be good (for)
Ser de rigor	842	Be indispensable, required by custom
Ser mal recibido	463	Be not well taken or received
Ser mano	971	Be first, lead out
Ser menester	875	Be necessary
Ser preciso	601	Be necessary, imperative
Ser un decir	799	Be just a myth, saying, manner of speaking
Ser una perla	894	Be a jewel or treasure
Serle a uno igual	428	Be all the same to one
Serle a uno indiferente	537	Make no difference to one, be immaterial
Servir para	522	Be used or useful for
Siempre armar líos	805	Always make trouble, raise a rumpus habitually
Sin embargo	214	However, nevertheless
Sin falta	119	Without fail
Sin faltar una jota	940	In minutest detail
Sin fin (de)	661	Endless, no end (of), numberless
Sin medida	633	Without moderation, to excess
Sin ningún género de duda	885	Without any doubt, beyond a shadow of a doubt
Sin novedad	462	As usual; nothing new, no news
Sin parar	427	Without a break, endlessly
Sin perjuicio de	718	Without affecting adversely
Sin ponderación	939	Without the slightest exaggeration

Sin qué ni para qué	951	Without any reason, cause, or motive
Sin querer	40	Unwittingly, unintentionally
Sin remedio	99	Hopeless, beyond solution
Sin reposo	903	Ceaselessly, endlessly
Sin ton ni son	479	Without rhyme or reason
Sobre la marcha	952	Simultaneously
Sobre todo	98	Especially
Suceda lo que suceda	331	Come what may, no matter what
Sudar la gota gorda	353	Have a bad time, sweat blood

Tal vez	16	Perhaps, probably, perchance
Tan pronto como	97	As soon as, the moment that
Tanto como	56	As much as
Tanto mejor	547	So much the better
Tanto peor	547	So much the worse
Tarde o temprano	96	Sooner or later, eventually
Tener a gala	996	Be proud of, take pride in
Tener a raya	660	Keep within bounds, control, restrain
Tener al corriente (de)	375	Keep someone posted or informed (about)
Tener antipatía	400	Dislike (someone), have an aversion (for someone)
Tener buen ojo	504	Have a good eye or good foresight
Tener confianza con	373	Be on intimate terms with
Tener cuidado	8	Be careful, watchful
Tener deseos de	90	Want to, be eager to
Tener detenido (algo)	798	Be holding (something) up
Tener disposición	728	Have aptitude or talent
Tener eco	785	Spread, catch on, become popular

SPANISH	FREQ.	ENGLISH
Tener en cuenta	276	Keep in mind, consider
Tener en la punta de la lengua	275	Have on the tip on one's tongue
Tener en la mente	584	Have in mind
Tener en poco	991	Hold in low esteem, be scornful of
Tener entre ceja y ceja	750	Dislike, have a grudge against
Tener fama de	274	Have the reputation of
Tener fe en	213	Believe or have faith in
Tener ganas de	74	Feel like, desire
Tener gracia	481	Be funny, witty
Tener ilusiones (de)	503	Have hopes, prospects, or illusions (of)
Tener la culpa	73	Be to blame
Tener la intención de	374	Intend or mean to
Tener la mira puesta en	870	Aim at, have as a goal
Tener la pena de	807	Have the misfortune to
Tener los huesos molidos	600	Be exhausted
Tener lugar	212	Take place, be held, occur
Tener mercado con	893	Trade with
Tener (mucho) mundo	813	Be sophisticated or experienced
Tener pesar	797	Be sorry for or about
Tener precisión	938	Need (to), have (to)
Tener presente	426	Bear or keep in mind
Tener prisa	461	Be in a hurry
Tener razón	118	Be right, correct
Tener relación con	478	Have connection with, have relation to
Tener retraso	536	Be late, be behind schedule
Tener sin cuidado	460	Care less, care not at all
Tener sus más y sus menos	961	Have one's good and bad points
Tener trazas	859	Show signs, give indications
Tocante a	925	About, touching on
Tocar de oído	372	Play by ear

SPANISH	FREQ.	ENGLISH
Tocar en lo vivo	959	Hurt (one) deeply, cut to the quick
Tocarle a uno	241	Be one's turn; concern one
Todas las veces que	211	Whenever, every time
Todavía no	94	Not yet
Todo bicho viviente	945	Every living soul, everyone under the sun
Todo lo contrario	273	Just the opposite, the other way around
Todo lo demás	298	Everything else
Todo lo posible	632	Everything possible, one's utmost
Tomar a broma	312	Take lightly or as a joke
Tomar a pecho	330	Take seriously or to heart
Tomar cuerpo	806	Take shape
Tomar el gusto	704	Take a liking to, grow fond of
Tomar el pelo	117	To deceive, pull one's leg (colloq.)
Tomar el rábano por las hojas	892	Put the cart before the horse
Tomar mala voluntad	826	Have a grudge against
Tomar medidas	240	Take measurements; take measures or steps
Tomar nota de	272	Take note of, jot down
Tomar parte	583	Take part
Tomarla con	866	Pick at or on, have a grudge against
Tomarle la palabra a una persona	727	Take a person at his word
Tomarse el trabajo de	631	Take the trouble to, be good enough to
Tomarse la libertad de	459	Take the liberty to
Trabajar como una fiera	917	Work like a dog
Trabar amistad	736	Strike up a friendship
Traer de cabeza a uno	949	Drive one crazy
Traer retraso	536	Be late, be behind schedule
Tropezar con	329	Run onto, encounter

Spanish	Freq.	English
Un no sé qué	403	A certain something
Uno que otro	659	Occasional(ly), some, a few
Unos cuantos	352	Some, a few

Spanish	Freq.	English
Valer la pena	7	Be worth(while), profitable
Valerse de	371	Make use of, avail one's self of
Variar de (or **en**) **opinión**	825	Change one's mind
Velar por	703	Take care of, protect
Venir a parar	311	Turn out, end up
Venirse abajo or **venirse a tierra**	567	Collapse, fall (through), fail
Ver visiones	161	See things, have false notions

Spanish	Freq.	English
Y así sucesivamente	116	And so on, et cetera
Y pico	115	And some odd (as in numbers), and something
Ya lo creo	328	Of course, certainly

PART 3
ENGLISH ALPHABETICAL LISTING

The system here is similar to that used in the Spanish alphabetical listing in part two: the frequency-of-occurrence number again refers the reader to more complete information in part one; the same word-by-word method has been followed; variant forms of the same expression are handled similarly, with separate listings unless they are adjacent in the alphabetical list.

Where two or more Spanish idioms are synonymous, the identical English translations are listed in order of frequency of occurrence. For example, "a few — 352 — *unos cuantos*" appears ahead of "a few — 659 — *uno que otro*." Where identical translations have different meanings, however, as in the case of "about (i.e., more or less)" and "about (i.e., with reference to)," each is followed by additional words or phrases clarifying the difference, and listed alphabetically accordingly.

ENGLISH	FREQ.	SPANISH

A

ENGLISH	FREQ.	SPANISH
A certain something	403	**Un no sé qué**
A few	352	**Unos cuantos**
A few	659	**Uno que otro**
A few lines	685	**Cuatro letras**
A kind of	902	**A modo de**
A laughing matter	544	**Cosa de risa**
A little after	141	**Poco después (de)**
A long time	502	**Largos años**
A sort of	902	**A modo de**
Abound with	721	**Rebozar de** (or **en**)
About, almost	455	**Cerca de**
About (i.e., more or less)	712	**Cosa de**
About (i.e., more or less)	838	**Poco más o menos**
About (i.e., with reference to)	310	**Acerca de**
About (i.e., with reference to)	645	**Con relación a**
About (i.e., with reference to)	925	**Tocante a**
About the middle of (week, month, etc.)	235	**A mediados de**
Above	355	**Por encima de**
Above all	98	**Sobre todo**

ENGLISH	FREQ.	SPANISH
Above all	614	**Ante todo**
Abroad	89	**En el extranjero**
Abruptly	321	**De pronto**
Absent one's self from	49	**Faltar a**
Accomplish	553	**Llevar a cabo**
According as	846	**Según y conforme** (or **como**)
According to	930	**Con arreglo a**
According to desire	795	**A pedir de boca**
According to my understanding	832	**A** (or **según**) **mi entender**
According to one's judgment or way of thinking	662	**Según el criterio de uno**
Account for	613	**Dar cuenta de**
Accustom one's self to	640	**Habituarse a**
Acknowledge (a person) to be right	269	**Dar la razón**
Acknowledge receipt of	457	**Acusar recibo de**
Across (the street)	37	**De enfrente**
Across the way from	590	**Enfrente de**
Across, through	646	**A través de**
Act as if	443	**Hacer de cuenta** (**que**)
Act like	628	**Conducirse como**
Act the fool	197	**Hacerse el tonto**
Address (i.e., speak)	346	**Dirigir la palabra**
Adequately	654	**De lleno**
Affect	933	**Rezar con**
After	135	**Después de**
After all	517	**Al fin y al cabo**
Again	10	**Otra vez**
Again	24	**De nuevo**
Agitate	106	**Poner el grito en el cielo**
Agree	66	**Estar de acuerdo**
Agree on	120	**Quedar en**
Agree to	483	**Quedar en** or **de**
Agree (with)	269	**Dar la razón**
Aided by	519	**A favor de**
Aim at (i.e., have as a goal)	870	**Tener la mira puesta en**

112

ENGLISH	FREQ.	SPANISH
All at once	149	**De la noche a la mañana**
All dressed up	975	**De punta en blanco**
All of a sudden	147	**De repente**
All of a sudden	321	**De pronto**
All of a sudden	673	**De golpe**
All out	865	**A todo**
All right	1	**Está bien** or **está bueno**
All right	891	**En hora buena**
All right then	618	**Pues bien**
All the better	926	**Mejor que mejor**
All the time	772	**A cada instante**
Almost	58	**Por poco**
Almost	455	**Cerca de**
Along	749	**A lo largo de**
Always make trouble, confusion, or difficulties	805	**Siempre armar líos**
Among	636	**Por entre**
Amount to, find one's self forced to	680	**Reducirse a**
Amount to (in money)	456	**Escender a**
And so	265	**De modo que**
And so	774	**Por lo cual**
And so doing	935	**Diciendo y haciendo**
And so on	116	**Y así sucesivamente**
And some odd (as in numbers), and something	115	**Y pico**
Anew	24	**De nuevo**
Anger (verb)	151	**Dar rabia**
Annoy	849	**Dar la lata**
Another time	10	**Otra vez**
Another time	24	**De nuevo**
Any time now	672	**De hoy a mañana**
Any way you look at it	932	**A todas luces**
Anyhow, anyway	880	**Así como así**
Anyway	530	**En todo caso**
Apologize for	308	**Disculparse por**

English	Freq.	Spanish
Apparently	41	**Por lo visto**
Apparently	464	**Según parece**
Apparently	716	**Al parecer**
Apple of one's eye	677	**La miña de sus** (or **mis, tus,** etc.) **ojos**
Apply (a coat of paint, varnish, etc.)	231	**Dar una mano**
Arise	195	**Ponerse de pie**
Around here	122	**Por aquí cerca**
Around the middle of (week, month, etc.)	235	**A mediados de**
Arouse pity or regret	92	**Dar lástima**
As (i.e., at the same time as)	615	**A medida que**
As (i.e., in the capacity of)	450	**En calidad de**
As a general rule	378	**Por regla general**
As a joke	47	**En** (or **de**) **broma**
As a matter of fact	671	**De hecho**
As a matter of form	976	**Por fórmula**
As a result	472	**De manera que**
As a rule	524	**Por lo regular**
As an emissary of	145	**En representación de**
As far as . . . is concerned	663	**Por lo que respecta** (or **toca**) **a**
As far as possible	448	**En lo posible**
As follows	771	**A continuación**
As hard as possible	863	**A más no poder**
As if it were of no importance	769	**Como quién no dice nada**
As it seems	464	**Según parece**
As long as	505	**Puesto que**
As luck may have it	187	**A lo mejor**
As much as	56	**Tanto como**
As much as possible	448	**En lo posible**
As simply as all that	880	**Así como así**
As soon as	68	**En cuanto**
As soon as	97	**Tan pronto como**
As soon as possible	395	**Cuanto antes**
As soon as you would like	113	**Cuando quiera**

ENGLISH	FREQ.	SPANISH
As the best of them	953	**Como el más pintado**
As time goes by	642	**De día en día**
As to the rest	570	**Por lo demás**
As usual	462	**Sin novedad**
As with the best of them	953	**Como el más pintado**
Aside from this	570	**Por lo demás**
Ask for (a person)	26	**Preguntar por**
Ask to lend	101	**Pedir prestado**
Ask too much (of)	800	**Pretender demasiado (de)**
Assert one's self over	490	**Imponerse a**
Associate with	451	**Juntarse con**
Assume	758	**Dar por hecho**
Assume as a responsibility	909	**Echarse sobre las espaldas**
Assume responsibility for	83	**Encargarse de**
At a distance	296	**A lo lejos**
At all hazards	692	**A toda costa**
At any cost	877	**A todo trance**
At any rate	31	**De todas maneras**
At dawn, at daybreak	873	**Al romper el día** (or **el alba**)
At every moment	772	**A cada instante**
At first	114	**Al principio**
At first glance, at first sight	927	**Al primer golpe de vista**
At full speed	770	**A toda prisa**
At full speed	985	**A toda vela**
At great length	18	**Por extenso**
At heart	85	**En el fondo**
At intervals	822	**De trecho en trecho**
At last (i.e., finally)	139	**Por fin**
At last (i.e., finally)	157	**Al fin**
At last (i.e., in the long run)	948	**A la postre**
At least	27	**Por lo menos**
At least	564	**Al menos**
At most	543	**Cuando más**
At most	790	**A lo más**

ENGLISH	FREQ.	SPANISH
At once (i.e., now)	210	**Ahora mismo**
At once (i.e., now)	580	**Al minuto**
At once (i.e., simultaneously)	327	**A la vez**
At one's own risk	619	**Por cuenta y riesgo**
At present	855	**Hoy por hoy**
At present	965	**Al presente**
At that time	531	**En aquel entonces**
At the expense of	566	**A costa de**
At the last moment	159	**A última hora**
At the latest	138	**A más tardar**
At the most	543	**Cuando más**
At the most	790	**A lo más**
At the outset	114	**Al principio**
At the outside	543	**Cuando más**
At the present time	227	**En la actualidad**
At the rate of	693	**A razón de**
At the request of	760	**A petición de**
At the same time	952	**Sobre la marcha**
At the same time as	615	**A medida que**
At very close range	794	**A quemarropa**
Attend to	102	**Ocuparse de**
Attract attention	105	**Llamar la atención**
Avail one's self of	371	**Valerse de**
Avoid	303	**Librarse de**
Avoid	820	**Guardarse de**

Back out	394	**Echarse atrás**
Back up	810	**Dar marcha atrás**
Bad disposition	239	**Mal genio**
Bad-natured	911	**Mal inclinado**
Bad temper	239	**Mal genio**
Base one's opinion on	492	**Fundarse en**

ENGLISH	FREQ.	SPANISH
Be a fan of	242	**Ser aficionado a**
Be a jewel	894	**Ser una perla**
Be a matter of	396	**Consistir en**
Be a member or part of	255	**Formar parte de**
Be a question of	396	**Consistir en**
Be a treasure	894	**Ser una perla**
Be a yes-man	988	**Decir a todo amén**
Be able to beat or keep time (music)	606	**Saber llevar el compás**
Be about to	286	**Estar a punto de**
Be about to	444	**Estar en vísperas de**
Be about to	786	**Estar para**
Be advantageous	7	**Valer la pena**
Be advisable	291	**Convenirle a uno**
Be against	313	**Ponerse en contra de**
Be agreed (that)	131	**Estar** (or **quedar**) **entendido que**
Be ahead	385	**Llevar ventaja**
Be ahead	467	**Llevar la delantera**
Be alert	277	**Prestar atención**
Be all in	130	**Estar rendido**
Be all the same to one	206	**Darle a uno lo mismo**
Be all the same to one	428	**Serle a uno igual**
Be almost to	828	**Estar próximo a**
Be an avid follower of	242	**Ser aficionado a**
Be annoyed	429	**Sentirse molesto**
Be annoyed	555	**Estar frito**
Be anxious to	363	**Estarse muriendo por**
Be as one likes it	297	**Estar a gusto**
Be ashamed	95	**Darle a uno vergüenza**
Be at ease	297	**Estar a gusto**
Be at fault	73	**Tener la culpa**
Be at the mercy of, expense of	829	**Estar a merced de**
Be at the point of	286	**Estar a punto de**
Be attentive	8	**Tener cuidado**
Be aware of	152	**Darse cuenta de**

English	Freq.	Spanish
Be becoming	361	**Irle a uno bien**
Be behind schedule	536	**Tener** (or **traer**) **retraso**
Be bent on	626	**Empeñarse en**
Be beside one's self with joy	808	**No caber en sí de gozo**
Be bewildered	510	**Quedarse confundido**
Be beyond repair, help or recourse	315	**No tener remedio**
Be beyond someone's reach	509	**Estar fuera del alcance de alguien**
Be bordered by	142	**Limitar con**
Be bored to death, bored stiff	819	**Matar de aburrimiento**
Be born lucky	739	**Nacer parado**
Be bothered	429	**Sentirse molesto**
Be bothered by	696	**Inquietarse con, de** or **por**
Be bound to	528	**Estar destinado a**
Be bounded or bordered by	142	**Limitar con**
Be but a shadow of one's former self	140	**No ser ni la sombra de uno**
Be careful	8	**Tener cuidado**
Be certain	674	**Dar por cierto** (or **seguro**)
Be coaxed	280	**Hacerse rogar**
Be comfortable	297	**Estar a gusto**
Be completely tired out	955	**Estar agotado**
Be composed of	452	**Constar de**
Be concerned for or about	25	**Preocuparse por**
Be confused	510	**Quedarse confundido**
Be confused	609	**Hacerse un lío**
Be congenial	50	**Hacer buenas migas**
Be contented	297	**Estar a gusto**
Be correct	118	**Tener razón**
Be correct	611	**Estar en lo cierto**
Be correct	814	**Decir bien**
Be deeply involved in	200	**Estar muy metido en**
Be delicious	839	**Saber a gloria**
Be depleted	130	**Estar rendido**
Be destined to	528	**Estar destinado a**
Be determined to	626	**Empeñarse en**

English	Freq.	Spanish
Be difficult, hard	150	**Costar mucho trabajo**
(Be) difficult, uphill	844	**Cuesta arriba**
Be disappointed	666	**Llevarse un chasco**
Be disappointed	742	**Estar desengañado**
Be discreet	764	**Guardar reserva**
Be disheartened	862	**Andar** (or **ir**) **de capa caída**
Be disillusioned	742	**Estar desengañado**
Be distressing	401	**Ser de lamentar**
Be dumbfounded	571	**Perder el habla**
Be dying to	363	**Estarse muriendo por**
Be eager to	90	**Tener deseos de**
Be eagerly attentive to	175	**Entusiasmarse con**
(Be) easy, downhill	844	**Cuesta abajo**
Be enthusiastic about	175	**Entusiasmarse con**
(Be) even	186	**A mano**
Be even	556	**Estar** (or **quedar**) **en paz**
Be evident to one	309	**Constarle a uno**
Be exceedingly difficult	767	**Costar un triunfo**
Be exhausted	130	**Estar rendido**
Be exhausted	600	**Tener los huesos molidos**
Be exhausted	955	**Estar reventado**
Be expected to (i.e., obliged to)	684	**Haber de**
Be expecting	470	**Estar a la expectativa de**
Be experienced	813	**Tener** (**mucho**) **mundo**
Be fashionable	21	**Estar de moda**
Be favorably disposed toward	809	**Inclinarse a**
Be fed up with	494	**Estar hasta la coronilla de**
Be first	971	**Ser mano**
Be forewarned	257	**Estar prevenido**
Be fully aware	376	**Saber de sobra**
Be funny	481	**Tener gracia**
Be getting late	33	**Hacerse tarde**
Be glad about (something)	38	**Alegrase de**
Be good (for)	900	**Ser de provecho**

ENGLISH	FREQ.	SPANISH
Be good enough to	631	**Tomarse el trabajo de**
Be grateful	2	**Dar las gracias**
Be grateful for one's kindness	916	**Estar reconocido por las atenciones**
Be growing late	33	**Hacerse tarde**
Be guided by	624	**Guiarse por**
Be hapless	305	**Estar de malas**
Be happy about (something)	38	**Alegrarse de**
Be happy with	350	**Contentarse con**
Be hard	150	**Costar mucho trabajo**
Be harmful to one	107	**Hacerle daño a uno**
Be held	212	**Tener lugar**
Be held down or back	142	**Limitar con**
Be highly desirable	904	**Ser de la mayor conveniencia**
Be holding (something) up	798	**Tener detenido (algo)**
Be hurt	681	**Estar sentido**
Be ill at ease	542	**Estar a disgusto**
Be immaterial	537	**Serle a uno indiferente**
Be imperative	601	**Ser preciso**
Be impolite to one	998	**Hacerle un feo a uno**
Be importuned	280	**Hacerse rogar**
Be in a bad way	862	**Andar (or ir) de capa caída**
Be in a good frame of mind or mood	612	**Estar en buena disposición (or de buen humor)**
Be in a hurry	461	**Tener prisa**
Be in a hurry	589	**Estar con (or de) prisa**
Be in a hurry	715	**Andar de prisa**
Be in accord	123	**Ponerse de acuerdo**
Be in charge	202	**Estar a cargo**
Be in command	529	**Estar al mando**
Be in effect	445	**Estar en vigor**
Be in favor of	508	**Estar por**
Be in force	445	**Estar en vigor**
Be in good condition	908	**Estar en buen uso**

ENGLISH	FREQ.	SPANISH
Be in haste	715	**Andar de prisa**
Be in mourning	12	**Estar de luto**
Be in no mood for joking	901	**No estar de gracia** (or **para gracias**)
Be in one's hands	720	**Obrar en poder de**
Be in somebody else's shoes	652	**Estar** (or **hallarse**) **en el pellejo de otro**
Be in the hands of	720	**Obrar en poder de**
Be in the mood	967	**Estar de vena**
Be in the mood for	669	**Estar en plan de**
Be in the possession of	720	**Obrar en poder de**
Be in the right	984	**Estar en lo firme**
Be in the way	320	**Estar de sobra**
Be inclined to	809	**Inclinarse a**
Be indebted to	342	**Estar en deuda con**
Be indispensable	842	**Ser de rigor**
Be irritable	906	**Levantarse del lado izquierdo**
Be just a myth, saying, manner of speaking	799	**Ser** (**algo**) **un decir**
Be just about to	828	**Estar próximo a**
Be late	536	**Tener** (or **traer**) **retraso**
Be loose-tongued	840	**Írsele a uno la lengua**
Be lost from sight	124	**Perderse de vista**
Be lost in thought	878	**Abstraer(se) en**
Be made the scapegoat	857	**Pagar los vidrios rotos**
Be mistaken	338	**Estar en un error**
Be mistaken about (something)	35	**Equivocarse de**
Be mixed up in	609	**Hacerse un lío**
Be much esteemed	572	**No tener precio**
Be necessary	80	**Hacer falta**
Be necessary	601	**Ser preciso**
Be necessary	875	**Ser menester**
Be noised around	734	**Correr el rumor** [or **la voz**]
Be not well taken or received	463	**Ser mal recibido**
Be nothing but skin and bones	869	**Estar** [or **quedar**] **en los huesos**

ENGLISH	FREQ.	SPANISH
Be obliged to (i.e., indebted to)	342	**Estar en deuda con**
Be obliged to (i.e., expected to)	684	**Haber de**
Be obvious	568	**Saltar a la vista**
Be obvious	1000	**Caerse por** [or **de**] **su (propio) peso**
Be of importance to one	79	**Importarle a uno**
Be of the same opinion	66	**Estar de acuerdo**
Be offended	681	**Estar sentido**
Be on duty	258	**Estar de turno**
Be on guard	8	**Tener cuidado**
Be on intimate terms with	373	**Tener confianza con**
Be on the downgrade	862	**Andar** (or **ir**) **de capa caída**
Be on the eve of	444	**Estar en vísperas de**
Be on the fence	596	**Cruzarse de brazos**
Be on the lookout	995	**Estar a la mira**
Be on the lookout for	470	**Estar a la expectativa de**
Be on the road	285	**Estar de viaje**
Be one's affair	290	**Correr por cuenta de uno**
Be one's turn	241	**Tocarle a uno**
Be onto someone	910	**Conocerle a uno el juego**
Be out for	669	**Estar en plan de**
Be out of breath	956	**Echar los bofes**
Be out of luck	305	**Estar de malas**
Be out of one's wits	668	**Fuera de quicio**
Be out of someone's reach	509	**Estar fuera del alcance de alguien**
Be outspoken	314	**No tener pelos en la lengua**
Be overcome	808	**No caber en sí de gozo**
Be overcome (with)	779	**Estar embriagado por**
Be overly tired	600	**Tener los huesos molidos**
Be overwhelmed (by)	779	**Estar embriagado por**
Be peeved	681	**Estar sentido**
Be perplexed	510	**Quedarse confundido**
Be popular	21	**Estar de moda**
Be prepared	257	**Estar prevenido**

English	Freq.	Spanish
Be priceless	572	**No tener precio**
Be pro	508	**Estar por**
Be profitable	7	**Valer la pena**
Be promoted to	456	**Ascender a**
Be proud of	996	**Tener a gala**
Be punished undeservingly	857	**Pagar los vidrios rotos**
Be ready	257	**Estar prevenido**
Be regrettable	401	**Ser de lamentar**
Be relieved	191	**Quitarse un peso de encima**
Be required by custom	842	**Ser de rigor**
Be responsible for (a person)	245	**Responder por**
Be right	118	**Tener razón**
Be right	611	**Estar en lo cierto**
Be right	814	**Decir bien**
Be rumored	734	**Correr el rumor** [or **la voz**]
Be satisfied with	250	**Contentarse con**
Be scornful of	991	**Tener en poco**
Be self-evident	568	**Saltar a la vista**
Be self-evident	1000	**Caerse por** [or **de**] **su (propio) peso**
Be smart	21	**Estar de moda**
Be softhearted	845	**Ser blando de corazón**
Be sophisticated	813	**Tener (mucho) mundo**
Be sorry about	797	**Tener pesar**
Be sorry for	278	**Pesarle a uno**
Be sorry for	797	**Tener pesar**
Be speechless	571	**Perder el habla**
Be square	556	**Estar** (or **quedar**) **en paz**
Be stubborn	248	**No dar el brazo a torcer**
Be stylish	21	**Estar de moda**
Be suitable for	722	**Entrar bien**
Be superfluous	320	**Estar de sobra**
Be terribly sorry	189	**Sentir en el alma**
Be the disturbing element	856	**Dar la nota discordante**

English	Freq.	Spanish
Be the last straw	887	**Llenar** (or **colmar**) **la medida**
Be the troublesome element	856	**Dar la nota discordante**
Be to blame	73	**Tener la culpa**
Be to one's advantage	291	**Convenirle a uno**
Be too bad	401	**Ser de lamentar**
Be (too) bashful	95	**Darle a uno vergüenza**
Be (too) inquisitive, intrusive, prying, or nosy	65	**Meterse en lo que no le importa**
Be (too) shy	95	**Darle a uno vergüenza**
Be traveling	285	**Estar de viaje**
Be trustworthy	634	**Ser de fiar**
Be unbecoming	361	**Irle a uno mal**
Be uncomfortable	542	**Estar a disgusto**
Be understood (that)	131	**Estar** (or **quedar**) **entendido que**
Be unreserved in speech	314	**No tener pelos en la lengua**
Be unwilling to	635	**Resistirse a**
Be unyielding	248	**No dar el brazo a torcer**
Be up to one	290	**Correr por cuenta de uno**
Be upset	554	**Incomodarse por**
Be used or useful for	522	**Servir para**
Be valuable	572	**No tener precio**
Be very busy	715	**Andar de prisa**
Be watchful	8	**Tener cuidado**
Be wearing	223	**Llevar puesto**
Be well mannered	602	**Ser correcto**
Be well taken or received	463	**Ser bien recibido**
Be with it (colloq.)	244	**Saber lo que es bueno**
Be witty	481	**Tener gracia**
Be worth(while)	7	**Valer la pena**
Be worthwhile	252	**Merecer la pena**
Be wrong	338	**Estar en un error**
Be wrong about (something)	35	**Equivocarse de**
Bear in mind	426	**Tener presente**

Beat around the bush	912	**Andarse por las ramas**
Become	506	**Llegar a ser**
Become angry	554	**Incomodarse por**
Become aware of	259	**Enterarse de**
Become involved with	868	**Identificarse con**
Become late	33	**Hacerse tarde**
Become popular	785	**Tener eco**
Before	263	**En presencia de**
Before tomorrow	672	**De hoy a mañana**
Beforehand	63	**Por adelantado**
Beforehand	209	**Con tiempo**
Begin, burst out	886	**Romper a**
Begin, burst out (laughing, crying, etc.)	261	**Echarse a (reír, llorar,** etc.)
Begin to	217	**Ponerse a**
Beginning now	287	**Desde ahora**
Behave as if	628	**Conducirse como**
Behave well	439	**Observar buena conducta**
Behind	86	**Detrás de**
Behind one's back	435	**Por detrás**
Behind the scenes	907	**Entre bastidores**
Behind the times	533	**Atrasado de noticias**
Believe in	213	**Tener fe en**
Below (i.e., as follows)	771	**A continuación**
Beside one's self	815	**Fuera de sí**
Bet everything	442	**Jugarse el todo por el todo**
Better half, spouse	621	**Media naranja**
Better off	682	**Más valiera**
Better yet	104	**Mejor dicho**
Between	636	**Por entre**
Beyond	253	**Más allá (de)**
Beyond a shadow of a doubt	885	**Sin ningún género de duda**
Beyond solution	99	**Sin remedio**
Binding	766	**En firme**
Bit by bit	20	**Poco a poco**

English	Freq.	Spanish
Blindly	616	**A ciegas**
Block the way	491	**Impedir el paso**
Blush	301	**Ponerse colorado**
Boast	729	**Hacer alarde**
Boast of	446	**Enorgullecerse de**
Boast of	941	**Preciarse de**
Bordering	749	**A lo largo de**
Borrow	101	**Pedir prestado**
Bother about	317	**Molestarse en**
Bother (i.e., annoy)	849	**Da la lata**
Bound for	369	**Con destino a**
Brag	729	**Hacer alarde**
Break into tears	830	**Deshacerse en lágrimas**
Break the thread (of a story)	782	**Cortar el hilo**
Briefly	593	**En concreto**
Briefly	743	**En unas cuantas palabras**
Briefly	812	**A grandes rasgos** (or **pinceladas**)
Brim over with	721	**Rebozar de** (or **en**)
Bring credit or discredit upon	719	**Reflejarse en**
Bring one up to date	357	**Poner a uno al corriente** (**de**)
Bring out	773	**Sacar a luz**
Bring suit or charges against	834	**Poner pleito**
Bring up, reveal	605	**Sacar a relucir**
Build castles in the air	731	**Forjarse ilusiones**
Build up goodwill	754	**Hacer méritos**
Buoy up	474	**Dar ánimo**
Burst out (laughing, crying, etc.)	261	**Echarse a** (**reír, llorar,** etc.)
Burst out, suddenly start to	886	**Romper a**
But	110	**En cambio**
Butt in	65	**Meterse en lo que no le importa**
By all means	932	**A todas luces**
By any means	322	**De ningún modo**
By chance	19	**Por casualidad**

ENGLISH	FREQ.	SPANISH
By dint of	566	**A costa de**
By dint of	582	**A fuerza de**
By elbowing	546	**A empujones**
By force	424	**A la fuerza**
By hand	186	**A mano**
By heart	5	**De memoria**
By means of	647	**Por intermedio de**
By nature	85	**En el fondo**
By no means	148	**De ninguna manera**
By no means	322	**De ningún modo**
By no means	649	**Ni en sueños**
By one's self	994	**Por sus puños**
By pushing, roughing, elbowing	546	**A empujones**
By the hundreds	921	**A centenares**
By the way	19	**Por casualidad**
By the way	91	**A propósito**
By what means?	347	**¿De dónde?**

Call attention to	105	**Llamar la atención**
Calm (i.e., presence of mind)	867	**Presencia de ánimo**
Care less, care not at all	460	**Tener sin cuidado**
Carry out	553	**Llevar a cabo**
Cast a glance	496	**Echar una ojeada**
Catch on	785	**Tener eco**
Cause	497	**Dar lugar a**
Cause annoyance	804	**Dar guerra**
Cause criticism	366	**Dar que decir** (or **hablar**)
Cause distress to	182	**Dar disgustos a**
Cause (extra) work	54	**Dar que hacer**
Cause grief to	182	**Dar disgustos a**
Cease	69	**Dejar de**
Ceaselessly	903	**Sin reposo**

ENGLISH	FREQ.	SPANISH
Censure	105	**Llamar la atención**
Certainly	121	**Por supuesto**
Certainly	328	**Ya lo creo**
Chance (verb)	183	**Correr riesgo**
Change one's mind	639	**Mudar** (or **cambiar**) **de opinión**
Change one's mind	825	**Variar de** (or **en**) **opinión**
Change the subject	918	**Doblar la hoja**
Charge a person with something	169	**Recomendar algo a uno**
Chatter	284	**Hablar hasta por los codos**
Cheat	578	**Dar gato por liebre**
Check (verb)	480	**Seguir los pasos a**
Cheer up	474	**Dar ánimo**
Chide	105	**Llamar la atención**
Choose (e.g., a profession)	575	**Meterse a**
Choose at random	732	**Esoger al azar**
Clash (e.g., colors)	883	**Contrastar mal**
Clear full	836	**Lleno de bote en bote**
Clear out	643	**Dar salida a**
Clear the table	777	**Levantar la mesa** [or **los mantels**]
Clear up, unravel	356	**Poner en claro**
Clear up, come to a conclusion	431	**Sacar en claro**
Collapse	567	**Venirse abajo** (or **venirse a tierra**)
Come hell or high water	691	**Contra viento y marea**
Come out ahead	243	**Salir ganando**
Come to a conclusion	431	**Sacar en claro**
Come to a mutual understanding or decision about	120	**Quedar en**
Come to an agreement	123	**Ponerse de acuerdo**
Come to grips with	511	**Enfrentarse con**
Come to (i.e., amount to)	680	**Reducirse a**
Come to pass	469	**Llegar a suceder**
Come to the point	414	**Dejarse de cuentos**

ENGLISH	FREQ.	SPANISH
Come to the point	686	**Dejarse de historias**
Come to the point	802	**Entrar en materia**
Come upon	329	**Tropezar con**
Come what may	331	**Suceda lo que suceda**
Come what may	691	**Contra viento y marea**
Comings and goings	623	**Idas y venidas**
Command respect from	490	**Imponerse a**
Complete	675	**Dar fin a**
Concentrate	878	**Abstraer (se) en**
Concern	933	**Rezar con**
Concern one	79	**Importarle a uno**
Concern one	241	**Tocarle a uno**
Concerning	310	**Acerca de**
Concerning	645	**Con relación a**
Concerning	925	**Tocante a**
Confine one's self to the subject	714	**Concretarse al tema**
Confront (i.e., face up to)	390	**Hacer frente a**
Confront	511	**Enfrentarse con**
Conscientiously	399	**A conciencia**
Consequently	550	**Por consiguiente**
Consider	276	**Tener en cuenta**
Consider	523	**Reflexionar sobre** [or **en**]
Consider	761	**Reparar en**
Consider one's self to be	485	**Presumir de**
Consist of	452	**Constar de**
Contend with	709	**Lidiar con**
Continued	771	**A continuación**
Contradict	489	**Llevar la contra**
Contrariwise	890	**A** (or **por**) **la inversa**
Contrive	627	**Darse maña**
Control	660	**Tener a raya**
Control one's tongue	827	**Morderse la lengua**
Cool (i.e., presence of mind)	867	**Presencia de ánimo**
Cope with	511	**Enfrentarse con**

ENGLISH	FREQ.	SPANISH
Correct	1	**Está bien** or **está bueno**
Cost plenty	498	**Costar un ojo de la cara**
Cost what it may	877	**A todo trance**
Count on	153	**Confiar en**
Count on	184	**Contar con**
Count on	337	**Fiar(se) en, a,** or **de**
Create a stir or sensation	753	**Meter** [or **hacer**] **ruido**
Criticize	962	**Cortar** (or **recortar**) **al prójimo**
Cross one's mind	30	**Ocurrírsele a uno**
Curriculum	170	**Plan de estudios**
Custom-made	422	**Hecho a la medida**
Cut out the nonsense	686	**Dejarse de historias**
Cut to the quick	959	**Tocar en lo vivo**

D

Darling	677	**La niña de sus** (or **mis, tus,** etc.) **ojos**
Dating from	23	**Desde hace**
Day by day	288	**De un día para otro**
Daydream	201	**Estar en las nubes**
Deceive	117	**Tomer el pelo**
Deceive	578	**Dar gato por liebre**
Deceive one's self	254	**Hacerse ilusiones**
Decide to	36	**Decidirse a**
Decline to	221	**Negarse a**
Deduce	548	**Sacar en limpio**
Definite	766	**En firme**
Delay	963	**Dar largas**
Deliberately	453	**Con intención**
Delude one's self	731	**Forjarse ilusiones**
Deny one's self	960	**Renunciar a sí mismo**
Depend upon	184	**Contar con**
Desire	74	**Tener ganas de**

Despite	271	**A pesar de**
Devolve upon	549	**Recaer sobre**
Digress	527	**Hacer un paréntesis**
Directly opposite	37	**De enfrente**
Disabuse someone	477	**Abrirle los ojos a uno**
Disappear	124	**Perderse de vista**
Discharge	515	**Dar de baja**
Discipline (verb)	860	**Meter en cintura**
Dislike	750	**Tener entra ceja y ceja**
Dislike (someone)	400	**Tener antipatía**
Dismiss	515	**Dar de baja**
Dispose of	643	**Dar salida a**
Distant from	224	**Lejos de**
Do a halfway job	469	**Hacer algo a medias**
Do a thing inadvertently	780	**Escapársele a uno**
Do marketing	11	**Ir de compras**
Do something poorly	469	**Hacer algo a medias**
Do without	622	**Pasarse sin**
Dominate	490	**Imponerse a**
Don't mention it	44	**No hay de qué**
Downhill	844	**Cuesta abajo**
Draw up plans	801	**Levantar planos**
Drive at, imply, mean	586	**Pretender decir**
Drive at, insinuate	348	**Dar a entender**
Drive one crazy	949	**Traer de cabeza a uno**
Drop (from a team, list, etc.)	515	**Dar de baja**
Drop (the matter)	982	**Correr** [or **echar**] **un velo (sobre)**

Earn a living	4	**Ganarse la vida**
Emphasize	699	**Hacer hincapié**
Emphasize	835	**Poner de relieve**
Encounter	329	**Tropezar con**

English	Freq.	Spanish
End up	311	**Venir a parar**
Endless	661	**Sin fin (de)**
Endlessly	427	**Sin parar**
Endlessly	903	**Sin reposo**
Enforce in a most conscientious fashion	980	**Poner en observancia**
Enjoy (e.g., health, comfort, rights)	514	**Disfrutar de**
Enjoy one's self	42	**Pasar un buen rato**
Enjoy your meal!	270	**¡Buen provecho!**
Entrust something to someone	169	**Recomendar algo a uno**
Equally	914	**Por igual**
Escape from	303	**Librarse de**
Escape one's attention	780	**Escapársele a uno**
Especially	98	**Sobre todo**
Especially	495	**En particular**
Esteem	173	**Hacer caso de**
Et cetera	116	**Y así sucesivamente**
Even	186	**A mano**
Evenly	914	**Por igual**
Eventually	96	**Tarde o temprano**
Eventually	565	**A la larga**
Ever since	136	**Desde que**
Every living soul	945	**Todo bicho viviente**
Every so often	234	**Alguna vez**
Every time	211	**Todas las veces que**
Everyone under the sun	945	**Todo bicho viviente**
Everything else	298	**Todo lo demás**
Everything possible	632	**Todo lo posible**
Evidently	41	**Por lo visto**
Exact time	532	**Hora fija**
Exactly	22	**En punto**
Exactly	593	**En concreto**
Exactly	977	**A punto fijo**
Exceed bounds	638	**Pasar de (la) raya**
Excel one's self	778	**Excederse a sí mismo**

Exhaust	613	**Dar cuenta de**
Express gratitude	2	**Dar las gracias**
Extend one's sympathy (for, on)	14	**Dar el pésame por**
Extreme	165	**Por las nubes**
Eye up and down	989	**Mirar de hito en hito**

Face down	232	**Boca abajo**
Face to face	109	**Frente a frente**
Face up to (i.e., confront)	390	**Hacer frente a**
Face up (to) (i.e., take the consequences)	689	**Dar la cara**
Face upward	232	**Boca arriba**
Facilitate	207	**Dar facilidades**
Fail, fall	567	**Venirse abajo** (or **venirse a tierra**)
Fall into the trap	931	**Caer en la red**
Fall or devolve upon	549	**Recaer sobre**
Fall through	567	**Venirse abajo** (or **venirse a tierra**)
Fancy (that)	493	**Figurarse que**
Far from	224	**Lejos de**
Far from it	466	**Ni mucho menos**
Far from it	792	**Ni soñar**
Far from it	986	**Ni con mucho**
Far removed from	224	**Lejos de**
Farther on (i.e., beyond)	253	**Más allá**
Farther on (i.e., further on, later)	488	**Más adelante**
Fashionable	398	**A la moda**
Favorably	534	**Con buenos ojos**
Feel like (i.e., want to)	74	**Tener ganas de**
Feel like (i.e., want to)	219	**Darle a uno la gana de**
Feel sorry for someone (or something)	324	**Compadecerse de alguien** (or **algo**)

English	Freq.	Spanish
Feel sure	674	**Dar por cierto** (or **serguro**)
Feel the lack or loss of	177	**Echar de menos**
Fewer than	127	**Menos de**
Fight with	866	**Tomarla con**
Finally (i.e., at last)	139	**Por fin**
Finally (i.e., at last)	157	**Al fin**
Finally (i.e., for the last time)	100	**Por última vez**
Find fault	962	**Cortar** (or **recortar**) **al prójimo**
Find one's self forced to	680	**Reducirse a**
Find out about	259	**Enterarse de**
Find out about	318	**Informarse de**
Find out where one stands	465	**Saber en qué se queda**
Fine	1	**Está bien** or **está bueno**
Finish	675	**Dar fin a**
Finish up	613	**Dar cuenta de**
Firm	766	**En firme**
Fit (verb)	722	**Entrar bien**
Follow (i.e., be guided by)	624	**Guiarse por**
Follow the current	724	**Dejarse llevar de la corriente**
Following	135	**Después de**
Fool one's self	254	**Hacerse ilusiones**
Foot the bill	172	**Pagar los gastos**
For (a certain time lapse)	23	**Desde hace**
For (i.e., in behalf of)	755	**En pro de**
For lack of	658	**A falta de**
For more than	512	**En más de**
For now	59	**Por ahora**
For such purpose	937	**A tal efecto**
For sure	977	**A punto fijo**
For that purpose	937	**A ese efecto**
For that reason	166	**Por eso**
For the first time	57	**Por primera vez**
For the future	393	**En lo futuro**
For the last time	100	**Por última vez**

ENGLISH	FREQ.	SPANISH
For the present	59	**Por ahora**
For the present	421	**Por hoy**
For the time being	434	**Por lo pronto**
For the time being	855	**Hoy por hoy**
For which reason	774	**Por lo cual**
For your guidance	957	**Para su gobierno**
Forcibly	424	**A la fuerza**
Forget	218	**Pasar por alto**
Forget a thing completely or entirely	968	**Quedársele a uno algo en el tintero**
Forget (to)	383	**Pasársele a uno**
Formal	230	**De etiqueta**
Fortunately	700	**Por fortuna**
Frankly	796	**A decir verdad**
Frequently	326	**A menudo**
From a distance, from afar	204	**Desde lejos**
From bad to worse	88	**De mal en peor**
From behind	435	**Por detrás**
From below	415	**Desde abajo**
From day to day	642	**De día en día**
From memory	5	**De memoria**
From now on	70	**De ahora en adelante**
From now on	112	**De aquí (or de hoy) en adelante**
From now on	287	**Desde ahora**
From one day to the next	288	**De un día para otro**
From the moment that	136	**Desde que**
From the outside	471	**Desde fuera**
From time to time	473	**De cuando en cuando**
Fruitlessly	84	**En vano**
Full dress	230	**De etiqueta**
Full to the brim	836	**Lleno de bote en bote**
Full-fledged	143	**Hecho y derecho**
Fully	15	**A carta cabal**
Fully	475	**A fondo**

Fully, adequately	654	**De lleno**
Fundamentally	592	**En principio**
Funny side	947	**Punto de gracia**
Furious(ly)	454	**Como una fiera**

Gain by	604	**Sacar partido de**
Gain from	617	**Sacar ventaja de**
Gather information on	318	**Informarse de**
Gesticulate	683	**Hacer gestos**
Get a lot out of	706	**Sacar jugo de**
Get along well together	50	**Hacer buenas migas**
Get along well with	128	**Llevarse bien con**
Get along with	332	**Quedar bien con**
Get along without	622	**Pasarse sin**
Get angry (about)	587	**Ponerse disgustado**
Get by, manage	569	**Salir del paso**
Get dark	389	**Hacerse de noche**
Get down to business	802	**Entrar en materia**
Get excited about	387	**Ilusionarse con**
Get gooseflesh	379	**Ponérsele a uno carne de gallina**
Get hurt	541	**Hacerse daño**
Get in a jam	609	**Hacerse un lío**
Get in touch with	419	**Comunicarse con**
[Get] in touch (with)	874	**Al habla (con)**
Get on one's feet	695	**Levantar cabeza**
Get one's due	111	**Empleársele bien a uno**
Get one's due	740	**Llevar su merecido**
Get one's own way	299	**Salirse con la suya**
Get out of the way	538	**Quitarse de en medio**
Get over (a state of mind)	383	**Pasársele a uno**
Get ready to	744	**Disponerse a** [or **para**]

ENGLISH	FREQ.	SPANISH
Get rid of	303	**Librarse de**
Get something back on someone	526	**Pagar en la misma moneda**
Get to be	506	**Llegar a ser**
Get to the point	409	**Ir al grano**
Get to work	905	**Ponerse a la obra**
Get up	195	**Ponerse de pie**
Get up on the wrong side of the bed	906	**Levantarse del lado izquierdo**
Get up one's hopes about	387	**Ilusionarse con**
Get upset about	696	**Inquietarse con, de** or **por**
Get what's coming	740	**Llevar su merecido**
Give account of	613	**Dar cuenta de**
Give aid	539	**Prestar ayuda**
Give an accounting to	162	**Rendir cuentas a** (or **ante**)
Give away	803	**Desprenderse de**
Give birth (to)	368	**Dar a luz**
Give free rein to	688	**Dar rienda suelta a**
Give in	936	**Doblar la cabeza**
Give indications	859	**Tener trazas**
Give information	655	**Dar razón**
Give (one) the runaround	963	**Dar largas**
Give one's condolences (for, on)	14	**Dar el pésame por**
Give one's self away	840	**Írsele a uno la lengua**
Give rein to	884	**Aflojar las riendas a**
Give rise to	497	**Dar lugar a**
Give tit for tat	526	**Pagar en la misma moneda**
Gladly	72	**Con mucho gusto**
Glory in	996	**Tener a gala**
Gloss over	218	**Pasar por alto**
Go along with the crowd	724	**Dejarse llevar de la corriente**
Go around something	154	**Dar la vuelta a algo**
Go blind	381	**Perder la vista**
Go fifty-fifty, go halves	196	**Ir a medias**
Go hunting for, go in search of	789	**Andar a caza de**
Go into reverse	810	**Dar marcha atrás**

ENGLISH	FREQ.	SPANISH
Go out to meet	705	**Salir al encuentro de**
Go over big	610	**Hacer furor**
Go over carefully	436	**Pasar revista a**
Go right by	540	**Pasar de largo**
Go shopping	11	**Ir de compras**
Go to the extreme	525	**Pasársele a uno la mano**
Go to waste	51	**Echar a perder**
Go too far	525	**Pasársele a uno la mano**
Go too far	638	**Pasar de (la) raya**
Go too far	778	**Excederse a sí mismo**
Go well, be becoming	361	**Irle a uno (bien)**
Go well together	768	**Contrastar bien**
Go well (with)	283	**Hacer juego**
Go without saying	1000	**Caerse por** [or **de**] **su (propio) peso**
Going to	369	**Con destino a**
Good	1	**Está bien** or **está bueno**
Good appetite!	270	**¡Buen provecho!**
Good bargain	384	**Negocio redondo**
Good nature or temper	239	**Buen genio**
Good-natured	911	**Bien inclinado**
Gradually	20	**Poco a poco**
Grasp (i.e., realize)	735	**Caer en la cuenta (de)**
Greatly	179	**De lo lindo**
Grow fond of	704	**Tomar el gusto**
Grown-up	143	**Hecho y derecho**
Guard against	820	**Guardarse de**
Guess (that)	493	**Figurarse que**

Half done	185	**A medio hacer**
Halfway (to a place)	518	**A medio camino**
Happen	468	**Llegar a suceder**

English	Freq.	Spanish
Harmonize	768	**Contrastar bien**
Harp on the same string	641	**Estar siempre con la misma cantaleta**
Hasten	702	**Apretar el paso**
Hastily	423	**A la carrera**
Hastily	883	**Por encima**
Have a bad time	353	**Sudar la gota gorda**
Have a good eye	504	**Tener buen ojo**
Have a good time	42	**Pasar un buen rato**
Have a grudge against	750	**Tener entre ceja y ceja**
Have a grudge against	826	**Tomar mala voluntad**
Have a grudge against	866	**Tomarla con**
Have a hunch	843	**Latirle a uno**
Have a lead	385	**Llevar ventaja**
Have a mind to	340	**Estar con ánimo de**
Have a narrow escape	946	**Salvarse en una tabla**
Have a notion to	340	**Estar con ánimo de**
Have a one-track mind	641	**Estar siempre con la misma cantaleta**
Have a premonition	843	**Latirle a uno**
Have an aversion (for someone)	400	**Tener antipatía**
Have (an illness or discomfort)	82	**Estar con**
Have an influence on	697	**Influir sobre** (or **en**)
Have an opinion of or about	125	**Pensar de**
Have aptitude	728	**Tener disposición**
Have as a goal	870	**Tener la mira puesta en**
Have at one's disposal	344	**Disponer de**
Have connection with	478	**Tener relación con**
Have dealings with	402	**Relacionarse con**
Have enough of	494	**Estar hasta la coronilla de**
Have faith in	213	**Tener fe en**
Have false notions	161	**Ver visiones**
Have good foresight	504	**Tener buen ojo**
Have great talent, flair, or aptitude for	944	**Pintarse solo para**
Have hopes or illusions (of)	503	**Tener ilusiones** (**de**)

Have in mind	584	**Tener en la mente**
Have just	39	**Acabar de**
Have need of	80	**Hacer falta**
Have no rhyme or reason	573	**No tener pies ni cabeza**
Have on the tip of one's tongue	275	**Tener en la punta de la lengua**
Have one's good and bad points	961	**Tener sus más y sus menos**
Have one's own way	299	**Salirse con la suya**
Have prospects (of)	503	**Tener ilusiones (de)**
Have reference to	190	**Referirse a**
Have relation to	478	**Tener relación con**
Have talent	728	**Tener disposición**
Have the flavor of	482	**Saber a**
Have the lead	467	**Llevar la delantera**
Have the misfortune to	807	**Tener la pena de**
Have the reputation of	274	**Tener fama de**
Have (to)	938	**Tener precisión**
Have to deal with (annoying, vexing persons)	709	**Lidiar con**
Have to do with	933	**Rezar con**
Having to do with	310	**Acerca de**
Having to do with	365	**En cuanto a**
Heading up	500	**Al frente de**
Heads or tails	657	**Cara o cruz**
Hear about, hear tell of	62	**Oír hablar de**
Heed	48	**Hacer caso a**
Help	539	**Prestar ayuda**
Help out	793	**Echar una mano** or **dar una mano**
Henceforth	112	**De aquí** (or **de hoy**) **en adelante**
Hereafter	393	**En lo futuro**
Hit	367	**Dar en**
Hit the ceiling	106	**Poner el grito en el cielo**
Hit the nail on the head, hit the mark	513	**Dar en el clavo**
Hold back	860	**Meter en cintura**
Hold in low esteem	991	**Tener en poco**

English	Freq.	Spanish
Hold one's tongue	827	**Morderse la lengua**
Hopeless	99	**Sin remedio**
How?	347	**¿De dónde?**
However	214	**Sin embargo**
However it be	597	**Como quiera que sea**
However much	246	**Por más que**
However much it may displease him (or me, you, etc.)	973	**Mal que le** (or **me, te,** etc.) **pese**
Humiliate	302	**Poner en ridículo**
Hurriedly	423	**A la carrera**
Hurry, hasten	702	**Apretar el paso**
Hurry, move quickly	323	**Darse prisa**
Hurry, speed up	823	**Apresurar la marcha**
Hurt (i.e., be harmful to) one	107	**Hacerle daño a uno**
Hurt (one) deeply	959	**Tocar en lo vivo**
Hurt one's self	541	**Hacerse daño**
Hush (something) up	982	**Correr** [or **echar**] **un velo** (**sobre**)

I

English	Freq.	Spanish
Identify one's self with	868	**Identificarse con**
If by chance	163	**Por si acaso**
If not	229	**De lo contrario**
If . . . not	250	**Mientras no**
If you don't mind	292	**Con permiso**
Ignorant of common things	533	**Atrasado de noticias**
I'll bet . . .	319	**A que...**
Ill-disposed	911	**Mal inclinado**
Imagine (that)	493	**Figurarse que**
Immediately afterwards	771	**A continuación**
Imply	586	**Pretender decir**
In a few words	743	**En unas cuantas palabras**
In a few words	812	**A grandes rasgos** (or **pinceladas**)

ENGLISH	FREQ.	SPANISH
In a jiffy	260	**En un dos por tres**
In a line	133	**En fila**
In a little while	87	**Dentro de poco**
In (a period of time)	53	**Dentro de**
In a soft voice	176	**En voz baja**
In a very short time	392	**En un abrir y cerrar de ojos**
In a way	449	**En cierta manera** (or **forma**)
In a way . . . in another way	192	**Por un lado... por otro**
In a word	144	**En resumidas cuentas**
In accordance with	181	**De acuerdo con**
In accordance with	644	**Conforme a**
In accordance with	930	**Con arreglo a**
In addition to	295	**Además de**
In advance	63	**Por adelantado**
In advance	209	**Con tiempo**
In agreement with	181	**De acuerdo con**
In any case, however it be	597	**Como quiera que sea**
In any event	31	**De todas maneras**
In any event	530	**En todo caso**
In back of	86	**Detrás de**
In behalf (of)	343	**En favor**
In behalf of	519	**A favor de**
In behalf of	755	**En pro de**
In brief	879	**En suma**
In charge of	500	**Al frente de**
In conformity with	181	**De acuerdo con**
In detail	18	**Por extenso**
In detail	484	**Punto por punto**
In detail	560	**Con detalle**
In every possible way	841	**En todos los tonos**
In every respect	15	**A carta cabal**
In exchange for	238	**A cambio de**
In fact	345	**En efecto**
In fact	671	**De hecho**

English	Freq.	Spanish
In favor of	519	**A favor de**
In favor of	755	**En pro de**
In front of	34	**Frente a**
In front (of)	37	**De enfrente**
In front of	52	**Delante de**
In front of	263	**En presencia de**
In front of	590	**Enfrente de**
In full regalia	975	**De punta en blanco**
In general	300	**Por lo general**
In good faith	180	**De buena fe**
In (good) time	209	**Con tiempo**
In great detail	598	**Al por menor**
In (great) style	599	**A lo grande**
In half	216	**Por la mitad**
In jest	47	**En** (or **de**) **broma**
In large quantity	156	**Al por mayor**
In leisure hours	997	**A ratos perdidos**
In light of	954	**A la luz de**
In line	133	**En fila**
In minutest detail	940	**Sin faltar una jota**
In my opinion	717	**A mi ver**
In my opinion	832	**A** (or **según**) **mi entender**
In my (or your, etc.) own way	458	**A mi** (or **tu, su,** etc.) **modo**
In one way or another	595	**De un modo u otro**
In order	411	**En regla**
In order that	501	**A fin de que**
In other words	174	**Es decir**
In outline	812	**A grandes rasgos** (or **pinceladas**)
In passing	417	**De paso**
In place of	67	**En lugar de**
In principle	592	**En principio**
In relation to	645	**Con relación a**
In round numbers	558	**En números redondos**
In shirt sleeves	262	**En mangas de camisa**

ENGLISH	FREQ.	SPANISH
In short	144	**En resumidas cuentas**
In short	306	**En fin**
In short	591	**En total**
In short	879	**En suma**
In so many words	593	**En concreto**
In spare time	997	**A ratos perdidos**
In spite of	271	**A pesar de**
In strictest confidence	783	**Con** (or **bajo**) **la mayor reserva**
In style	398	**A la moda**
In such a case or instance	341	**En tal caso**
In the act	499	**Con las manos en la masa**
In the capacity of	450	**En calidad de**
In the center	132	**En la mitad**
In the dark, blindly	616	**A ciegas**
In the distance	296	**A lo lejos**
In the end	517	**Al fin y al cabo**
In the event that	163	**Por si acaso**
In the event that	208	**Con tal que**
In the first place	203	**En primer lugar**
In the future	70	**De ahora en adelante**
In the future	393	**En lo futuro**
In the light of	954	**A la luz de**
In the long run	565	**A la larga**
In the long run	948	**A la postre**
In the meantime	64	**Mientras tanto**
In the meantime	434	**Por lo pronto**
In the middle	216	**Por la mitad**
In the middle of	132	**En`la mitad** (de)
In the nick of time	159	**A última hora**
In the presence of	52	**Delante de**
In the twinkling of an eye	392	**En un abrir y cerrar de ojos**
In the vicinity	122	**Por aquí cerca**
In this manner	205	**De esta manera** (or **este modo**)
In trade for	238	**A cambio de**

English	Freq.	Spanish
In transit	417	**De paso**
In vain	84	**En vano**
Inadvertently say or do a thing	780	**Escapársele a uno**
Incidentally	19	**Por casualidad**
Incomplete	185	**A medio hacer**
Influence (verb)	697	**Influir sobre** (or **en**)
Inform	268	**Dar parte**
Inform one	357	**Poner a uno al corriente** (**de**)
Informal	559	**De confianza**
Initially	114	**Al principio**
Inquire about (a person)	26	**Preguntar por**
Inside	168	**Por dentro**
Inside (of)	53	**Dentro de**
Inside out	55	**Al revés**
Insignificant	45	**Lo de menos**
Insinuate	348	**Dar a entender**
Insist on	762	**Obstinarse en**
Insist upon	699	**Hacer hincapié**
Instead of	67	**En lugar de**
Instead of	108	**En vez de**
Instead of	650	**Mejor que**
Intend	3	**Pensar en**
Intend to	374	**Tener la intención de**
Interrupt	782	**Cortar el hilo**
Intimate	559	**De confianza**
It appears to be impossible	43	**Parece mentira**
It depends	846	**Segun y conforme** (or **como**)
It doesn't matter	763	**No le hace**
It hardly seems possible	43	**Parece mentira**
It is known that	919	**Es fama que**
It is necessary, obligatory, or required to (that)	9	**Hay que**
It is said or rumored that	919	**Es fama que**
It makes no difference	763	**No le hace**

Jest	293	**Burlarse de**
Join (e.g., a military unit, a society)	576	**Incorporarse a**
Jot down	272	**Tomar nota de**
Judging by appearances	41	**Por lo visto**
Judging from or by	678	**A juzgar por**
Just	39	**Acabar de**
Just about	58	**Por poco**
Just as it is	562	**Así nada más**
Just in case	163	**Por si acaso**
Just, just now	210	**Ahora mismo**
Just like that	880	**Así como así**
Just plain	562	**Así nada más**
Just the opposite	273	**Todo lo contrario**
Just the opposite	821	**El reverso de la medalla**

Keep an eye on	480	**Seguir los pasos a**
Keep from	820	**Guardarse de**
Keep in mind	276	**Tener en cuenta**
Keep in mind	426	**Tener presente**
Keep one's mouth shut, keep silent	776	**No despegar los labios**
Keep someone posted or informed (about)	375	**Tener al corriente (de)**
Keep within bounds	660	**Tener a raya**
Kill time	126	**Pasar el rato**
Kill time	405	**Matar el tiempo**
Kill two birds with one stone	407	**Matar dos pájaros de** [or **en**] **un tiro**
Kindest regards to	708	**Muchos recuerdos a**
Kneel down	577	**Hincarse de rodillas**
Know perfectly or by heart	679	**Saber al dedillo**

English	Freq.	Spanish
Know what is going on	244	**Saber lo que es bueno**
Know what one is missing	244	**Saber lo que es bueno**
Knowingly	453	**Con intención**

L

English	Freq.	Spanish
Lack	80	**Hacer falta**
Land, make a stop	391	**Hacer escala**
Late at night	974	**Muy noche**
Late in (week, month, etc.)	236	**A fines de**
Later on	488	**Más adelante**
Lay the blame on	267	**Echar la culpa a**
Lead into error	851	**Inducir a error**
Lead out, be first	971	**Ser mano**
Learn about	259	**Enterarse de**
Leastwise	27	**Por lo menos**
Leave alone	137	**Dejar en paz**
Leave no stone unturned	928	**No dejar piedra por** (or **sin**) **mover**
Leave one high and dry	416	**Dejarle a uno plantado**
Leave one indifferent	871	**No darle a uno frío ni calor**
Leave one in the lurch	416	**Dejarle a uno plantado**
Leave word	266	**Dejar dicho**
Lend a hand	539	**Prestar ayuda**
Lend a hand	793	**Echar una mano**
Lend an ear	876	**Dar oídos**
Lend itself to	433	**Prestarse a**
Lengthwise of	749	**A lo largo de**
Less than	127	**Menos de**
Lest	335	**No sea que**
Let be	137	**Dejar en paz**
Let something out (by talking)	840	**Írsele a uno la lengua**
Let something slip	780	**Escapársele a uno**
Let's get to work!	359	**¡Manos a la obra!**
Like a wild beast	454	**Como una fiera**

Like as not	187	**A lo mejor**
Like (i.e., similar to)	60	**Parecido a**
Like manna from heaven	629	**Como llovido del cielo**
Line up	29	**Hacer cola**
Listen	876	**Dar oídos**
Listen intently	958	**Aguzar los oídos** [or **el oído**]
Listen to reason	853	**Atender razones**
Little by little	20	**Poco a poco**
Little by little	664	**Paso a paso**
Live in luxury	751	**Nadar en la abundancia**
Lock the door	787	**Echar la llave**
Lofty (in price or praise)	165	**Por las nubes**
Long for	177	**Echar de menos**
Look after	818	**Mirar por**
Look around	487	**Mirar alrededor**
Look askance at, look down upon	896	**Mirar de lado**
Lose one's head, lose one's cool	279	**Perder la cabeza**
Lose one's vision	381	**Perder la vista**
Lose sight of	358	**Perder de vista**
Lose the thread of	382	**Perder el hilo de**
Luckily	891	**En hora buena**

Made to order or measure	422	**Hecho a la medida**
Mail (letters, etc.) (verb)	307	**Echar al correo**
Make a final or clean copy	637	**Poner en limpio**
Make a fool of	302	**Poner en ridículo**
Make a gift of	608	**Obsequiar con**
Make a good showing	225	**Hacer buen papel**
Make a great fuss	106	**Poner el grito en el cielo**
Make a hit	610	**Hacer furor**
Make a hit (i.e., get along) with	332	**Quedar bien con**
Make a living	4	**Ganarse la vida**

Make a noise	753	**Meter** [or **hacer**] **ruido**
Make a poor showing	225	**Hacer mal papel**
Make a special request of someone for something	169	**Recomendar algo a uno**
Make a stop	391	**Hacer escala**
Make an effort to recall or remember	698	**Hacer memoria**
Make (extra) work	54	**Dar que hacer**
Make faces (at)	683	**Hacer gestos**
Make fun of	293	**Burlarse de**
Make furious	151	**Dar rabia**
Make gestures (at)	683	**Hacer gestos**
Make heads or tails of	548	**Sacar en limpio**
Make insinuations	653	**Echar indirectas**
Make known	656	**Dar a conocer**
Make mention of	507	**Hacer referencia a**
Make no difference to one	537	**Serle a uno indiferente**
Make noise	753	**Meter** (**hacer**) **ruido**
Make objections	817	**Poner reparo**(s)
Make one angry	711	**Darle a uno coraje**
Make one blush	915	**Hacerle salir los colores a uno**
Make one sorry	155	**Dar mucha pena**
Make one's self deserving	754	**Hacer méritos**
Make one's way	535	**Abrirse paso** (or **camino**)
Make payments	61	**Pagar a plazos**
Make stand out	835	**Poner de relieve**
Make trouble	804	**Dar guerra**
Make unreasonable demands (on)	800	**Pretender demasiado** (**de**)
Make up for	924	**Resarcirse de**
Make up one's mind to	36	**Decidirse a**
Make use of	371	**Valerse de**
Manage (i.e., contrive)	627	**Darse maña**
Manage (i.e., get by)	569	**Salir del paso**
Manage (skillfully) to	730	**Ingeniárselas para**
Manage to	563	**Arreglárselas para**
Manifest sorrow for a death	12	**Estar de luto**

ENGLISH	FREQ.	SPANISH
Many years	502	**Largos años**
Mark one's word	81	**Fijarse en**
Match (verb)	283	**Hacer juego**
Matter to one	79	**Importarle a uno**
Mature	143	**Hecho y derecho**
Maybe	16	**Tal vez**
May you profit from your food!	270	**¡Buen provecho!**
Mean	17	**Querer decir**
Mean, imply	586	**Pretender decir**
Mean to	374	**Tener la intención de**
Meanwhile	64	**Mientras tanto**
Melt into tears	830	**Deshacerse en lágrimas**
Mention	773	**Sacar a luz**
Miss (i.e., absent one's self from)	49	**Faltar a**
Miss (i.e., long for)	177	**Echar de menos**
Miss (i.e., not notice)	780	**Escapársele a uno**
Miss the mark	765	**Errar el tiro**
More or less	712	**Cosa de**
More or less	838	**Poco más o menos**
More than	512	**En más de**
Move cautiously	561	**Caminar con pies de plomo**
Move quickly	323	**Darse prisa**
Much ado about nothing	934	**Mucho ruido y pocas nueces**
Mumble	594	**Decir** (or **hablar**) **entre dientes**
Muse	201	**Estar en las nubes**
Mutter	594	**Decir** (or **hablar**) **entre dientes**

ENGLISH	FREQ.	SPANISH
Namely	920	**A saber**
Naturally	413	**Desde luego**
Near (location)	455	**Cerca de**
Nearby	186	**A mano**
Nearly	58	**Por poco**

Nearly	455	**Cerca de**
Nearsighted	545	**Corto de vista**
Need (to)	938	**Tener precisión**
Never mind	763	**No le hace**
Nevertheless	214	**Sin embargo**
Nip in the bud	690	**Cortar de raíz**
No buts about it!	441	**¡No hay pero que valga!**
No end (of)	661	**Sin fin (de)**
No matter how hard one tries	551	**Ni para remedio**
No matter how much	246	**Por más que**
No matter what	164	**Por ningún motivo**
No matter what	331	**Suceda lo que suceda**
No matter what happens	31	**De todas maneras**
No news	462	**Sin novedad**
No sooner said than done	476	**Dicho y hecho**
Nor anything like it	466	**Ni mucho menos**
Not a single	249	**Ni siquiera**
Not agree (physically) with one	107	**Hacerle daño a uno**
Not any place	194	**Por ningún lado** [or **ninguna parte**]
Not be a laughing matter	316	**No ser cosa de juego**
Not be able to stand, endure, control, manage	336	**No poder con**
Not be able to stand the sight of	76	**No poder ver ni en pintura**
Not be able to tolerate someone	103	**No poder ver a alguien**
Not by any means, not by a long shot	792	**Ni soñar**
Not by any means, not by a long shot	986	**Ni con mucho**
Not even	249	**Ni siquiera**
Not for anything	574	**Ni a tiros**
Not for love or money	551	**Ni para remedio**
Not for love or money	574	**Ni a tiros**
Not get along with	332	**Quedar mal con**
Not [know] in the slightest	983	**Ni por el forro**
Not know which way to turn	404	**No saber dónde meterse**

English	Freq.	Spanish
Not make a hit with	332	**Quedar mal con**
Not make heads or tails, not make sense	573	**No tener pies ni cabeza**
Not mince words	858	**No morderse la lengua**
Not notice	780	**Escapársele a uno**
Not yet	94	**Todavía** [or **aún**] **no**
Nothing new	462	**Sin novedad**
Nothing special, nothing unusual	222	**Nada de particular**
Notice	761	**Reparar en**
Notice	929	**Echar de ver**
Notify	268	**Dar parte**
Notify of	741	**Hacer presente**
Now and then	234	**Alguna vez**
Now then	630	**Ahora bien**
Nowadays	388	**Hoy en día** or **hoy día**
Nowhere	194	**Por ningún lado** [or **ninguna parte**]
Numberless	661	**Sin fin** (**de**)

English	Freq.	Spanish
Obey	48	**Hacer caso a**
Object (verb)	489	**Llevar la contra**
Observe	761	**Reparar en**
Observe	929	**Echar de ver**
Obstruct the way	491	**Impedir el paso**
Occasionally	473	**De cuando en cuando**
Occasional(ly)	659	**Uno que otro**
Occur	212	**Tener lugar**
Occur to one (i.e., cross one's mind)	30	**Ocurrírsele a uno**
Odds and/or evens	588	**Pares o** (or **y**) **nones**
Of course, certainly	121	**Por supuesto**
Of course, certainly	328	**Ya lo creo**
Of course, naturally	413	**Desde luego**
Of importance	745	**De categoría**

Of importance	864	**De peso**
Of little importance	45	**Lo de menos**
Of one's own accord	247	**Por las buenas**
Off the record	899	**A título de información**
Offer to	433	**Prestarse a**
Offer every assistance	207	**Dar facilidades**
Offer resistance	438	**Oponer resistencia**
Often	326	**A menudo**
OK	1	**Está bien** or **está bueno**
OK	891	**En hora buena**
On a large scale	723	**En grande**
On behalf (of)	343	**En favor**
On hand (money)	625	**En caja**
On its side	418	**De lado**
On one's back	232	**Boca arriba**
On one's own	994	**Por sus puños**
On one's stomach	232	**Boca abajo**
On purpose	91	**A propósito**
On purpose	943	**De intento**
On that occasion	531	**En aquel entonces**
On the average	430	**Por término medio**
On the condition that	520	**A condición de que** or **con la condición de que**
On the contrary	158	**Al contrario**
On the contrary	890	**A** (or **por**) **la inversa**
On the dot	22	**En punto**
On the exterior	77	**Por fuera**
On the inside	168	**Por dentro**
One the one side (or hand) . . . on the other	192	**Por un lado... por otro**
On the other hand	110	**En cambio**
On the other hand	158	**Al contrario**
On the other hand	193	**Por otra parte**
On the outside	77	**Por fuera**
On the request of	760	**A petición de**

English	Freq.	Spanish
On the run	423	**A la carrera**
On the understanding that	520	**A condición de que** or **con la condición de que**
On top of	339	**En lo alto de**
Once and for all	816	**De una vez y para siempre**
Once more	10	**Otra vez**
Once more	24	**De nuevo**
One-way	824	**De dirección única** or **de un solo sentido**
One's utmost	632	**Todo lo posible**
Open someone's eyes	477	**Abrirle los ojos a uno**
Oppose	313	**Ponerse en contra de**
Oppose	489	**Llevar la contra**
Opposite (i.e., across the way from)	590	**Enfrente de**
Opposite (i.e., contrary)	55	**Al revés**
Or else, lest	335	**No sea que**
Or rather	104	**Mejor dicho**
Ordinarily	300	**Por lo general**
Ordinarily	524	**Por lo regular**
Otherwise	229	**De lo contrario**
Out loud	176	**En voz alta**
Out of date	171	**Pasado de moda**
Out of one's wits	668	**Fuera de quicio**
Out of style	171	**Pasado de moda**
Out of the clear blue sky	552	**Llovido del cielo**
Out of the country	89	**En el extranjero**
Outdo one's self	778	**Excederse a sí mismo**
Outshine	882	**Prevalecer sobre**
Over	355	**Por encima de**
Over a period of	23	**Desde hace**
Overdo	525	**Pasársele a uno la mano**
Overlook	218	**Pasar por alto**
Overnight	149	**De la noche a la mañana**
Overstep	778	**Excederse a sí mismo**

English	Freq.	Spanish
Painstakingly	399	**A conciencia**
Particularly	98	**Sobre todo**
Particularly	495	**En particular**
Pass by without stopping	540	**Pasar de largo**
Pass over (i.e., overlook)	218	**Pasar por alto**
Pass right by	540	**Pasar de largo**
Pass the time away	126	**Pasar el rato**
Passé	171	**Pasado de moda**
Pay attention	277	**Prestar atención**
Pay attention to (i.e., heed, obey)	48	**Hacer caso a**
Pay attention to (i.e., mark one's word)	81	**Fijarse en**
Pay attention to (i.e., take into account, respect)	173	**Hacer caso de**
Pay (close) attention	620	**Poner mucho ojo**
Pay in installments	61	**Pagar a plazos**
Pay the expenses	172	**Pagar los gastos**
Perchance	16	**Tal vez**
Perhaps	16	**Tal vez**
Persist in	626	**Empeñarse en**
Persist in	762	**Obstinarse en**
Pester	849	**Dar la lata**
Pick a fight with	281	**Meterse con**
Pick a quarrel	854	**Armar una bronca**
Pick at or on	866	**Tomarla con**
Pick out at random	732	**Escoger al azar**
Pity someone (or something)	324	**Compadecerse de alguien** (or algo)
Play a dirty trick on one	999	**Hacerle a uno un flaco servicio**
Play by ear	372	**Tocar de oído**
Play dumb	197	**Hacerse el tonto**
Play practical jokes	667	**Gastar bromas pesadas**

English	Freq.	Spanish
Please excuse me	292	**Con permiso**
Point-blank	794	**A quemarropa**
Point of view	215	**Punto de vista**
Point out	835	**Poner de relieve**
Poke fun at	293	**Burlarse de**
Politely	811	**Con buenos modos**
Pose a problem	607	**Plantear una dificultad**
Possibly	16	**Tal vez**
Post (letters, etc.) (verb)	307	**Echar al correo**
Pour (i.e., rain bucketfuls)	651	**Llover a cántaros** (or **chorros**)
Preferably	408	**Más bien**
Prepare one's self to	744	**Disponerse a** [or **para**]
Presence of mind	867	**Presencia de ánimo**
Present	608	**Obsequiar con**
Present a difficulty	607	**Plantear una dificultad**
Present one's condolences (for, on)	14	**Dar el pésame por**
Pretend	348	**Dar a entender**
Pretend not to see	752	**Hacer(se) (de) la vista gorda**
Pretend not to understand	648	**No darse por entendido**
Pretend (that)	443	**Hacer de cuenta** (**que**)
Pretend to be contemptuous of	969	**Hacer ascos de**
Prevail against or over	882	**Prevalecer sobre**
Prick up one's ears	775	**Parar la oreja**
Prick up one's ears	958	**Aguzar los oídos** [or **el oído**]
Pride one's self on	446	**Enorgullecerse de**
Print, publish	773	**Sacar a luz**
Probably	16	**Tal vez**
Procrastinate	963	**Dar largas**
Profit by	604	**Sacar partido de**
Profit by	617	**Sacar ventaja de**
Progressively	20	**Poco a poco**
Promise to	483	**Quedar en** or **de**
Proof against (e.g., fireproof)	581	**A prueba de**
Provided that	208	**Con tal que**

ENGLISH	FREQ.	SPANISH
Provided that	520	**A condición de que** or **con la condición de que**
Protect	703	**Velar por**
Provoke one	711	**Darle a uno coraje**
Publish	773	**Sacar a luz**
Pull one's leg (colloq.)	117	**Tomar el pelo**
Purely by chance	199	**De pura casualidad**
Push one's way in	897	**Entrar a empellones**
Put in final form or shape	831	**Dar forma a**
Put in motion	380	**Poner en marcha**
Put off	963	**Dar largas**
Put the cart before the horse	892	**Tomar el rábano por las hojas**

Q

Queue (up)	29	**Hacer cola**
Quickly	260	**En un dos por tres**
Quit	69	**Dejar de**

R

Rack one's brains	861	**Devanarse los sesos**
Rack one's brains	964	**Calentarse los cascos**
Rain bucketfuls	651	**Llover a cántaros** (or **chorros**)
Raise a rumpus habitually	805	**Siempre armar líos**
Raise objections	489	**Llevar la contra**
Raise objections	817	**Poner reparo(s)**
Rather, preferably	408	**Más bien**
Rather than	108	**En vez de**
Rather than	650	**Mejor que**
Read between the lines	942	**Leer entre renglones**
Realize	152	**Darse cuenta de**
Realize	735	**Caer en la cuenta (de)**
Reason	993	**Decir para sí**

English	Freq.	Spanish
Red-handed	499	**Con las manos en la masa**
Refer to	190	**Referirse a**
Refer to	507	**Hacer referencia a**
Reflect on (i.e., bring credit or discredit upon)	719	**Reflejarse en**
Reflect on (i.e., consider)	523	**Reflexionar sobre** [or **en**]
Refresh one's memory	354	**Refrescar la memoria**
Refuse to	221	**Negarse a**
Refuse to	635	**Resistirse a**
Refuse to consider	256	**Hacerse el sordo**
Regarding, having to do with	365	**En cuanto a**
Regret, be sorry for	278	**Pesarle a uno**
Regret deeply	189	**Sentir en el alma**
Relax watchfulness or authority over	884	**Aflojar las riendas a**
Reliable	178	**Digno de confianza**
Reluctantly	289	**De mala gana**
Reluctantly	898	**De mal grado**
Rely on	153	**Confiar en**
Rely on	337	**Fiar(se) en, a,** or **de**
Remain indifferent	596	**Cruzarse de brazos**
Remain with	75	**Quedarse con**
Remind of	741	**Hacer presente**
Render an accounting to	162	**Rendir cuentas a** (or **ante**)
Report	268	**Dar parte**
Representing	145	**En representación de**
Reprimand	105	**Llamar la atención**
Reputable	178	**Digno de confianza**
Resolve to	36	**Decidirse a**
Resort to	781	**Echar mano de**
Respect	173	**Hacer caso de**
Restrain	660	**Tener a raya**
Restrain	860	**Meter en cintura**
Retail	598	**Al por menor**
Rethink	694	**Recapacitar sobre**
Reveal (i.e., bring up)	605	**Sacar a relucir**

ENGLISH	FREQ.	SPANISH
Revert to (i.e., fall upon)	549	**Recaer sobre**
Review	436	**Pasar revista a**
Right	345	**En efecto**
Right away	210	**Ahora mismo**
Right away	580	**Al minuto**
Right from the start or beginning	226	**Desde un principio**
Right here	370	**Aquí mismo**
Right (in)	654	**De lleno**
Right now	227	**En la actualidad**
Right now	965	**Al presente**
Right (on)	654	**De lleno**
Right on time	532	**Hora fija**
Right side out	397	**Al derecho**
Right to a person's face	516	**Cara a cara**
Rotate something	154	**Dar la vuelta a algo**
Roughly (i.e., in round numbers)	558	**En números redondos**
Round-trip	28	**Ida y vuelta**
Rudely	811	**Con malos modos**
Ruin	51	**Echar a perder**
Run a risk	349	**Correr peligro**
Run an errand	282	**Hacer un mandado**
Run onto, encounter	329	**Tropezar con**
Run over in one's mind	694	**Recapacitar sobre**
Run risk	183	**Correr riesgo**

	FREQ.	SPANISH
Safely	891	**En hora buena**
Saunter	13	**Dar una vuelta**
Save time	362	**Ganar tiempo**
Say a thing inadvertently	780	**Escapársele a uno**
Say to one's self	993	**Decir para sí**
See the point of	735	**Caer en la cuenta (de)**
See things	161	**Ver visiones**

English	Freq.	Spanish
Seem strange to one	198	**Extrañarle a uno**
Seemingly	41	**Por lo visto**
Serve someone right	111	**Empleársele bien a uno**
Set of courses	170	**Plan de estudios**
Set on fire	333	**Prender fuego a**
Set out	738	**Ponerse en camino**
Set the table	6	**Poner la mesa**
Shake hands (with)	410	**Estrechar la mano (a)**
Share (in)	437	**Participar de**
Sharp	22	**En punto**
Sharpen one's wits	966	**Afilar** (or **aguzar**) **el ingenio**
Shortly	87	**Dentro de poco**
Show disrespect to	49	**Faltar a**
Show signs	859	**Tener trazas**
Show signs of	687	**Dar señales de**
Show signs or indications of	725	**Dar muestras de**
Shrug one's shoulders	557	**Encogerse de hombros**
Sideways	418	**De lado**
Similar to	60	**Parecido a**
Simultaneously	327	**A la vez**
Simultaneously	952	**Sobre la marcha**
Since, as long as	505	**Puesto que**
Since then, since that time	146	**Desde entonces**
Skip a line	759	**Comerse un renglón**
Sky-high	165	**Por las nubes**
Sleep on	713	**Consultar con la almohada**
Slight one	998	**Hacerle un feo a uno**
Slip away	922	**Escurrir el bulto**
Slip out of or through one's hands (or fingers)	888	**Escurrirse de entre las manos**
Slowly	20	**Poco a poco**
Sneak away	922	**Escurrir el bulto**
So	166	**Por eso**
So	265	**De modo que**

ENGLISH	FREQ.	SPANISH
So far	228	**Hasta aquí**
So much the better	926	**Mejor que mejor**
So much the better (worse)	547	**Tanto mejor (peor)**
So that	265	**De modo que**
So (that)	501	**A fin de que**
So that (i.e., as a result)	472	**De manera que**
So what	707	**Qué más da**
Some	352	**Unos cuantos**
Some	659	**Uno que otro**
Some fine day (ironic)	970	**El mejor día**
Somehow	595	**De un modo u otro**
Something is wrong	665	**Haber moros en la costa**
Something like that, something of the kind	294	**Algo por el estilo**
Something worthwhile or worth seeing	412	**Cosa (digna) de ver**
Sometimes	234	**Alguna vez**
Somewhere near here	122	**Por aquí cerca**
Soon	87	**Dentro de poco**
Soon after	141	**Poco después (de)**
Sooner or later	96	**Tarde o temprano**
Sooner or later	881	**A la corta o a la larga**
Sound bargain	384	**Negocio redondo**
Spare no efforts	850	**No omitir esfuerzos**
Speak	346	**Dirigir la palabra**
Speak straight from the shoulder	858	**No morderse la lengua**
Speak with outright frankness	788	**Cantar claro or cantárselas claras**
Specifically	174	**Es decir**
Specifically	920	**A saber**
Speed up	823	**Apresurar la marcha**
Spend	344	**Disponer de**
Spoil	51	**Echar a perder**
Spoil things	923	**Echar(lo) todo a rodar**
Spouse	621	**Media naranja**
Spread	785	**Tener eco**

English	Freq.	Spanish
Sprint	701	**Dar una carrera**
Squander	344	**Disponer de**
Squarely, right (in, on)	654	**De lleno**
Stand	195	**Ponerse de pie**
Stand in line	29	**Hacer cola**
Stand someone up	416	**Dejarle a uno plantado**
Stand the cost	172	**Pagar los gastos**
Stand up to	511	**Enfrentarse con**
Standpoint	215	**Punto de vista**
Stare at	847	**Mirar con fijeza**
Stare at	989	**Mirar de hito en hito**
Start	380	**Poner en marcha**
Start a fight	854	**Armar una bronca**
Start a row	753	**Meter** [or **hacer**] **ruido**
Start out	738	**Ponerse en camino**
Start out to	217	**Ponerse a**
Stay with	75	**Quedarse con**
Step by step, in detail	484	**Punto por punto**
Step by step, little by little	664	**Paso a paso**
Stop	69	**Dejar de**
Stop beating around the bush	414	**Dejarse de cuentos**
Stop beating around the bush, making excuses, temporizing	670	**Dejarse de rodeos**
Strike one (as) funny	304	**Hacer gracia**
Strike up a friendship	736	**Trabar amistad**
Strive hard to	889	**Extremarse en**
Strive to	364	**Esforzarse en, por,** or **para**
Stumble upon	329	**Tropezar con**
Suddenly	673	**De golpe**
Suddenly	710	**De buenas a primeras**
Suddenly start to	886	**Romper a**
Suddenly start to (laugh, cry, etc.)	261	**Echarse a**
Sue	585	**Proceder en contra**
Sue	834	**Poner pleito**

ENGLISH	FREQ.	SPANISH
Superficially	833	**Por encima**
Surely	972	**De fijo**
Surpass	882	**Prevalecer sobre**
Surround one's self with	432	**Rodearse de**
Sweat blood	353	**Sudar la gota gorda**
Sympathize with someone (or something)	324	**Compadecerse de alguien** (or **algo**)

T

ENGLISH	FREQ.	SPANISH
Take a firm stand against	699	**Hacer hincapié**
Take a liking to	704	**Tomar el gusto**
Take a load off one's mind	191	**Quitarse un peso de encima**
Take a nap	733	**Echar un sueño**
Take a person at his word	727	**Tomarle la palabra a una persona**
Take a quick look	496	**Echar una ojeada**
Take a stroll	13	**Dar una vuelta**
Take a walk or stroll	233	**Dar un paseo**
Take action against	585	**Proceder en contra**
Take advantage of the situation	325	**Aprovechar la ocasión**
Take as a joke	312	**Tomar a broma**
Take (as in choosing or buying)	75	**Quedarse con**
Take care of, attend to	102	**Ocuparse de**
Take care of, look after	818	**Mirar por**
Take care of, protect	703	**Velar por**
Take charge of	83	**Encargarse de**
Take for granted	758	**Dar por hecho**
Take for granted	913	**Dar por descontado**
Take into account	173	**Hacer caso de**
Take lightly	312	**Tomar a broma**
Take measurements	240	**Tomar medidas**
Take measures or steps	240	**Tomar medidas**
Take note of, jot down	272	**Tomar nota de**
Take note of, realize	735	**Caer en la cuenta (de)**

Take on	909	**Echarse sobre las espaldas**
Take part	583	**Tomar parte**
Take place	212	**Tener lugar**
Take precautions against	377	**Prevenirse contra**
Take pride in	941	**Preciarse de**
Take pride in	996	**Tener a gala**
Take seriously	330	**Tomar a pecho**
Take shape	806	**Tomar cuerpo**
Take steps (i.e., measures)	240	**Tomar medidas**
Take the consequences (of)	689	**Dar la cara**
Take the intervening day off	979	**Hacer puente**
Take the liberty to	459	**Tomarse la libertad de**
Take the trouble to	317	**Molestarse en**
Take the trouble to	631	**Tomarse el trabajo de**
Take to	367	**Dar en**
Take to heart	330	**Tomar a pecho**
Take upon one's self (e.g., a profession)	575	**Meterse a**
Talk for the sake of talking	848	**Decir por decir**
Talk idly	284	**Hablar hasta por los codos**
Taste like	482	**Saber a**
Tell one	357	**Poner a uno al corriente (de)**
Tell one (so)	264	**Advertir algo a alguien**
Tell straight from the shoulder	788	**Cantar claro** or **cantárselas claras**
Thank	2	**Dar las gracias**
Thanks to	188	**Gracias a**
That far	747	**A tal punto**
That is	174	**Es decir**
That is	920	**A saber**
That is to say	174	**Es decir**
That which is stated, directed, or requested	360	**Lo indicado**
The bulk (of)	46	**La mayor parte (de)**
The coast is not clear	665	**Haber moros en la costa**
The contrary	55	**Al revés**

ENGLISH	FREQ.	SPANISH
The first part of (a time period, e.g., month, year)	748	**A principios de**
The less . . . the less	251	**Mientras menos... menos**
The less . . . the less	579	**Cuanto menos... menos**
The majority (of)	46	**La mayor parte (de)**
The moment that	68	**En cuanto**
The moment that	97	**Tan pronto como**
The more . . . the more	251	**Mientras más... más**
The more . . . the more	579	**Cuanto más... más**
The opposite	55	**Al revés**
The opposite in every respect	821	**El reverso de la medalla**
The other way around	273	**Todo lo contrario**
The other way around	890	**A** (or **por**) **la inversa**
There are no two ways about it	440	**No hay que darle vueltas**
There is more than meets the eye	420	**Hay gato encerrado**
Therefore	166	**Por eso**
Therefore	550	**Por consiguiente**
There's no doubt or uncertainty (that)	406	**No cabe duda (de que)**
There's nothing to do but	220	**No hay más remedio que**
There's where the trouble lies	852	**En eso estriba la dificultad**
These days	388	**Hoy en día** or **hoy día**
Think about	3	**Pensar en**
Think nothing of it	44	**No hay de qué**
Think of (i.e., about or over)	3	**Pensar en**
Think of (i.e., have an opinion about)	125	**Pensar de**
Think of one's self as	485	**Presumir de**
Think on	735	**Caer en la cuenta (de)**
Think over	3	**Pensar en**
Think over	523	**Reflexionar sobre** [or **en**]
Think over	713	**Consultar con la almohada**
This way	205	**De esta manera** (or **este modo**)
Thoroughly	15	**A carta cabal**
Thoroughly	351	**Al pie de la letra**
Thoroughly	475	**A fondo**

English	Freq.	Spanish
Through (i.e., across)	646	**A través de**
Through (i.e., among)	636	**Por entre**
Through (i.e., by means of)	647	**Por intermedio de**
Throw one's self into a job	956	**Echar los bofes**
Tied to the apron-strings of	950	**Cosido a las faldas de**
Time agreed upon	532	**Hora fija**
To a certain point or extent	129	**Hasta cierto punto**
To date	32	**Hasta la fecha**
To excess	633	**Sin medida**
To one's self	895	**Para el interior de uno**
To such end	937	**A tal efecto**
To sum up	591	**En total**
To tell the truth (i.e., frankly)	796	**A decir verdad**
To that end	937	**A ese efecto**
To the best of my knowledge	978	**Según mi leal saber y entender**
To the discredit of	981	**En mengua de**
To the limit	865	**A todo**
To the point of	746	**Al extremo de**
To the utmost	863	**A más no poder**
Too much, too many	71	**De más**
Touching on	925	**Tocante a**
Toward the end of (week, month, etc.)	236	**A fines de**
Track down, trace	603	**Seguir el rastro**
Trade with	893	**Tener mercado con**
Treasure	677	**La niña de sus** (or **mis, tus,** etc.) **ojos**
Trust in	153	**Confiar en**
Trust in	337	**Fiar(se) en, a,** or **de**
Trustworthy	178	**Digno de confianza**
Turn something	154	**Dar la vuelta a algo**
Turn a deaf ear	256	**Hacerse el sordo**
Turn out	311	**Venir a parar**
Turn up one's nose at	969	**Hacer ascos de**

Two-way	28	**Ida y vuelta**

Under any circumstances	322	**De ningún modo**
Under full sail	985	**A toda vela**
Under no circumstances	148	**De ninguna manera**
Under no circumstances	164	**Por ningún motivo**
Under no circumstances	322	**De ningún modo**
Under observation	447	**En observación**
Understand	548	**Sacar en limpio**
Unexpectedly	147	**De repente**
Uniformly	914	**Por igual**
Unintentionally	40	**Sin querer**
Unless	250	**Mientras no**
Unless	726	**A menos que**
Unofficially	899	**A título de información**
Unravel	356	**Poner en claro**
Unthinkable	649	**Ni en sueños**
Unwillingly	289	**De mala gana**
Unwillingly	898	**De mal grado**
Unwittingly	40	**Sin querer**
Up to now	32	**Hasta la fecha**
Up to now	228	**Hasta aquí**
Uphill	844	**Cuesta arriba**
Upon returning from	791	**A la vuelta de**
Upset everything carelessly	923	**Echar(lo) todo a rodar**
Use discretion	764	**Guardar reserva**
Usually	300	**Por lo general**
Usually	378	**Por regla general**

Valuable	572	**No tener precio**

ENGLISH	FREQ.	SPANISH
Vanish	124	**Perderse de vista**
Very much	179	**De lo lindo**
Vouch for (a person)	245	**Responder por**

W

ENGLISH	FREQ.	SPANISH
Walk	13	**Dar una vuelta**
Walk arm in arm	78	**Ir del brazo**
Want to	90	**Tener deseos de**
Want to	219	**Darle a uno la gana**
Waste time	405	**Matar el tiempo**
Way of getting on with people	757	**Don de gentes**
Way over there	296	**A lo lejos**
Weak side or spot	386	**Lado flaco**
Wear	223	**Llevar puesto**
Weighty, of importance	864	**De peso**
Well (expletive)	306	**En fin**
Well now	630	**Ahora bien**
Well-disposed	911	**Bien inclinado**
What is the date today?	784	**¿A cuánto(s) estamos?**
Whatever the cost	692	**A toda costa**
What's the difference	707	**Qué más da**
When least expected	872	**En un descuido**
When one least expects	134	**El día menos pensado**
When you are ready	113	**Cuando quiera**
When you least expect it	674	**De hoy a mañana**
Whence?	347	**¿De dónde?**
Whenever	211	**Todas las veces que**
Whenever you would like	113	**Cuando quiera**
Where?	167	**¿Por dónde?**
Whether he (or I, you, etc.) likes it or not	973	**Mal que le** (or **me, te,** etc.) **pese**
Whether one likes it or not	334	**Por las buenas o por las malas**
Which is why	774	**Por lo cual**
Which way?	167	**¿Por dónde?**

English	Freq.	Spanish
Wholesale	156	**Al por mayor**
Wide open	237	**Abierto de par en par**
Willingly	72	**Con mucho gusto**
Willingly	247	**Por las buenas**
Willingly	289	**De buena gana**
Win	243	**Salir ganando**
Wind (a watch, clock, toy)	93	**Dar cuerda a**
Wink at	752	**Hacer(se) (de) la vista gorda**
Winning manners	757	**Don de gentes**
Wish	14	**Tener ganas de**
With, aided by	519	**A favor de**
With certainty	977	**A punto fijo**
With complete confidence	180	**De buena fe**
With good manners	811	**Con buenos modos**
With great difficulty	160	**A duras penas**
With great haste	770	**A toda prisa**
With great pleasure	72	**Con mucho gusto**
With little effort	987	**A poca costa**
With no confidence	180	**De mala fe**
With pleasure	289	**De buena gana**
With poor manners	811	**Con malos modos**
With reference or regard to	310	**Acerca de**
With reference or regard to	645	**Con relación a**
With reference or regard to	925	**Tocante a**
With respect to, with regard to	521	**Con respecto a**
With the help of	647	**Por intermedio de**
With the intention of	990	**A reserva de**
With the object or purpose of	676	**Con objeto de**
With vivid description	992	**A lo vivo**
With your permission	29	**Con permiso**
Withdraw	394	**Echarse atrás**
Within	168	**Por dentro**
Within (a period of time)	53	**Dentro de**
Within a short time	756	**En breve plazo**

ENGLISH	FREQ.	SPANISH
Within reach	186	**A mano**
Without a break, endlessly	427	**Sin parar**
Without affecting adversely	718	**Sin perjuicio de**
Without any cause	951	**Sin qué ni para qué**
Without any doubt	885	**Sin ningún género de duda**
Without any reason or motive	951	**Sin qué ni para qué**
Without doubt	972	**De fijo**
Without fail	119	**Sin falta**
Without moderation	633	**Sin medida**
Without reason	880	**Así como así**
Without restraint	837	**A rienda suelta**
Without rhyme or reason	479	**Sin ton ni son**
Without the knowledge of	425	**A escondidas de**
Without the slightest exaggeration	939	**Sin ponderación**
Without warning	710	**De buenas a primeras**
Wonder if, when, how, etc.	486	**Preguntarse si, cuándo, cómo,** etc.
Wonderfully	179	**De lo lindo**
Word for word, thoroughly	351	**Al pie de la letra**
Work hard	956	**Echar los bofes**
Work like a dog	917	**Trabajar como una fiera**
Workday	737	**Día hábil**
Worry about	25	**Preocuparse por**
Worry about	696	**Inquietarse con, de,** or **por**
Wrong side out	55	**Al revés**

Yield	936	**Doblar la cabeza**
You're welcome	44	**No hay de qué**

APPENDIX 1

Facsimile of Page One
of List Evaluated by Native Speakers

J. Dale Miller
Regional Language Supervisor
American Embassy Mexico

*Nicaragua
Roberto Arana*

LISTA DE MIL EXPRESIONES IDIOMATICAS

Se le suplica revisar la presente lista de más de mil expresiones idiomáticas de acuerdo con las instrucciones. Tenga especial cuidado de asignar a cada una de ellas la relativa frecuencia de ocurrencia que usted crea sea la apropiada.

Si usted conoce algún sinónimo a forma equivalente de cualquiera de estas expresiones que sea de uso común en su país, le agradecería lo anotara precisamente arriba de la expresión correspondiente. Sin embargo, se debe tener cuidado de que las adiciones sugeridas no rayen en lo vulgar.

Agradezco de antemano su asistencia, con la cual está usted contribuyendo al asesoramiento profesional que ayudará a las personas de habla inglesa en su aprendizaje del idioma español.

		De Uso Frecuente en su País SI	NO	Frecuencia Relativa*
1.	A bien or a buen librar If everything turns out all right, if nothing happens	A buen librar llegaremos mañana en la noche.		×	
2.	A cada instante All the time, constantly, at every moment	A cada instante esperan estallar una insurrección.	×		2
3.	A cambio de In exchange for	Le daré este libro a cambio de ese otro.	×		4
4.	A carta cabal Thoroughly, in every respect	Es honrado a carta cabal.	×		2
5.	A centenares By hundreds	Murieron las gentes a centenares.	×		1
6.	A ciegas In the dark, blindly	Se metió en ese negocio a ciegas.	×		2
7.	A conciencia Conscientiously, painstakingly	Hizo su trabajo a conciencia.	×		4
8.	A condición de que, con la condición de que On the understanding that, on condition that, provided that	Iré a condición de que Ud. vaya conmigo.	×		4

*Póngase el número apropiado:
  Por una expresión de frecuencia alta, 4
  Por una expresión de frecuencia corriente, 3
  Por una expresión de frecuencia regular, 2
  Por una expresión de frecuencia rara, 1

171

APPENDIX 2

Frequency Listing of Idioms

Frequency indicates numerical order 1 to 1,000. *Rating* gives the average "Frecuencia Relativa" for each expression as evaluated by checkers.

FREQ.	RATING	FREQ.	RATING	FREQ.	RATING
1	172	647–658	132	914–916	96
2–3	167	659–678	131	917–921	95
4–6	166	679–693	130	922–924	94
7–15	165	694–702	129	925–927	93
16–24	164	703–717	128	928–932	92
25–31	163	718–726	127	933–937	91
32–39	162	727–737	126	928–943	89
40–55	161	738–749	125	944	87
56–72	160	750–760	124	945–948	86
73–88	159	761–772	123	949–950	85
89–114	158	773–784	122	951	84
115–138	157	785–791	121	952–955	83
139–160	156	792–796	120	956–958	82
161–187	155	797–805	119	959–961	81
188–210	154	806–812	118	962–965	80
211–238	153	813–816	117	966	79
239–271	152	817–823	116	967–969	78
272–297	151	824–832	115	970–972	77
298–310	150	833–838	114	973–974	76
311–327	149	839–844	113	975–978	75
328–351	148	845–849	112	979	74
352–370	147	850–854	111	980	73
371–399	146	855–856	110	981	71
400–425	145	857–858	109	982–983	70
426–459	144	859–863	108	984–985	68
460–476	143	864–869	107	986	67
477–502	142	870–874	106	987	66
503–521	141	875–878	105	988–989	65
522–535	140	879–881	104	990–991	63
536–546	139	882–884	103	992–994	60
547–566	138	885–888	102	995	58
567–582	137	889–891	101	996	57
583–599	136	892–899	100	997	56
600–616	135	900–902	99	998	55
617–630	134	903–912	98	999	52
631–646	133	913	97	1000	49